S0-BAH-981

JUDGMENT

Copyright © 2014

Rice University School of Architecture

First Paperback Printing 2014

ISBN: 978-0-9899612-0-2

Published as #48 in the *Architecture at Rice* publication series.

Publisher:
Rice School of Architecture
Rice University MS-50
6100 Main Street
Houston, TX 77005
USA
T: 713-348-4864
F: 713-348-5277
E: arch@rice.edu
www.arch.rice.edu

Distribution:
Actar D
151 Grand Street, 5th Floor
New York, NY 10013
USA
T: 212-966-2207
F: 212-966-2214
E: salesnewyork@actar-d.com
www.actar-d.com

CONTENTS

Foreword

Sarah Whiting

The Future. Now.

Judgment.

It's such a weighty term for such a little book. Judgment seems so heavy, so fraught. Judgment takes on a bewildering aura when attention is drawn to it, like the doubt that develops when thinking too long about how to spell a word. Asking why a decision was made guarantees a frozen panic; for all of our earnest bluster, self-conscious doubts run deep in the waters of architectural production.

Judgment makes us uncomfortable because it's, well ... *judgmental.* Open-mindedness is a *de rigueur* personality trait for contemporary thinkers. No doubt, we have long reaped the benefits of ever expanding subjectivities: new topics, voices, disciplines, geographies, and politics have exponentially multiplied, establishing a richer and more beneficial world for all of us. To be judgmental seems utterly at odds with this expanded field. And yet, looking across architecture today, it strikes me that in our relentless pursuit of everything we have crossed the (invisible) line that separates proliferate good intentions from an avalanche of indiscriminacy. Does ever *more* equate with ever *better*? Has architecture advanced beyond what it was a year ago? A decade ago? A half-century ago? Have our cities become better? Have we enhanced our cultural present? Our prospective future?

Looking back gives pause to our suspended sense of judgment. The exhaustion of options has acquired an aura of something akin to intelligence. But prodigious output ought not be mistaken for conceptual consequence. And, far worse, might not the sheer multiplicity of our output be muffling more piercing and more urgently needed speculations about the future?

Architectural judgments radiate from reigning discourses. Across the twentieth century these discourses included technological optimism, good-life modernism, populism, environmentalism, and, for lack of a better term, brash capitalism. If the status quo felt stifling, one could always turn the status quo on its head. *Less is more* not to your taste? No problem — How about I whip you up a little *Less is a bore*? Camps, the easiest way of identifying oneself, are also the easiest means of breaking ranks, of moving on. Camps bother us today. Maybe that's because they're supposed to. But even if they're not meant to annoy us, flying flags with particular ideological colors is especially invigorating when it comes to progressive discourse. "I want to live here, not there" has come to signal vulnerability or even incorrectness. But isn't it precisely that kind of desire, a visceral subjectivity, that leads to a tomorrow that is better than today?

During the 2011-2012 school year, with these questions and ruminations as a backdrop, the Rice School of Architecture undertook a series of conversations around the subject of judgment. I invited an enthusiastic and (at times) contentious set of voices to take on our topic within the setting of the school: Markus Miessen, Hal Foster, Ben van Berkel, Neil Denari, Sylvia Lavin, Jeff Kipnis, Brett Steele, and R. E. Somol. In lectures and roundtable discussions, across dinners and drinks, my aim was to reinvigorate what it means to declare one's bias in architecture.

This book came out of those conversations. It is filled with clippings from countless exchanges that arose in formal and informal contexts across many days and evenings. The authors were extraordinarily gracious in consenting to let us man-handle their ideas in this way. Our intention was not so much to pin them down as it was to illuminate the full force of sentiments that arose around a subject, an illumination that depended on the comments, questionings, and alchemies of faculty, students, and visitors in the School of Architecture for its brightness. In addition to thanking the participants — those invited and those on the home team — and the Rice School of Architecture staff, who worked tirelessly to make the events appear effortless, I am extremely grateful to Scott Colman and Ron Witte for editing down hours and hours of material to these precise, provocative assertions: these judgments.

— Sarah Whiting, Dean, Rice School of Architecture

Post-Critical?

Hal Foster

Diatribe

I wrote for this occasion a diatribe about the post-critical. I understand this term has a particular valence in architectural discourse. It tends to wrap into a moment a period of theoretical reflexivity associated with architects like Peter Eisenman, to insist on a pragmatic relationship to design, and to insist on intelligence intrinsic to architecture. That will not be my concern here, for the most part. Rather, I address the term post-critical in its general sense.

Beating

Critical theory took a serious beating during the culture wars of the 1980s and 1990s.

Worse

The 2000s were only worse.

Bully

Bullied by conservative commentators, most academics no longer stress the importance of critical thinking for an engaged citizenry and, dependent on corporate sponsors, most curators will no longer promote a critical debate, once deemed essential to the public discussion of advanced art and architecture. Indeed, the datedness of criticism in a world that couldn't care less seems evident enough. But what are the options on offer? Celebrating beauty, affirming affect, hoping for a redistribution of the sensible?

Moral

How did we arrive at the point where critique is so broadly dismissed? Over the years, most of the charges have concerned the positioning of the critic. First, there was a rejection of judgment, of the moral right presumed in critical evaluation. Then there was a refusal of authority, of the political privilege that allows the critic to speak abstractly on behalf of others. Finally, there was skepticism about distance, about the cultural separation from the very conditions that the critic purports to examine.

"Criticism is a matter of correct distancing," Walter Benjamin wrote over eighty years ago. "It was at home in a world where perspectives and prospects counted and where it was still possible to adopt a standpoint. Now things press too urgently on human society."

How much more urgent is this pressing today?

Bathwater

As for the other old charges, which come mostly from the left, they boil down to two in the end: critique is driven by a will to power and is not reflexive about its own claims to truth.

Often enough two fears drive these two accusations, or they did in the formation of my generation: on the one hand, a concern about the critic as "ideological patron" who displaces the very group or class that he represents — this is the famous caution given by Walter Benjamin in his "Author as Producer" essay of 1934; and, on the other hand, a concern about the scientific truth ascribed to critical theory in opposition to "spontaneous ideology" — this is the dubious position that is assumed by Louis Althusser in his re-reading of Marx.

Such fears are not misbegotten, but are they reason enough to throw the baby out with the bathwater?

Shrug

The problem is not that truths are always hidden — I think Bruno Latour and Jacques Rancière are right here — but that many are all too apparent, yet with a transparency that somehow impedes, even blocks, our response. "I know the mantra of 'no taxes' is a boon to the rich, and a bust for me, but nevertheless …" "I know the big museums have more to do with finance capital than with public culture, but nevertheless …" As a fetishistic operation of recognition and disavowal — precisely: "I know, but nevertheless …" and not say it, see it, etc. — cynical reason is also subject to anti-fetishistic critique.

Of course, such critique is never enough: one must intervene in what is given, somehow turn it, and take it elsewhere. Yet that turning, I think, begins with critique. Maybe I am dead wrong: What about the blossoming of "critical art" today? We're beyond critical architecture; critical art, at least as a rubric, is still very much with us.

Friction

There's friction here, stemming from whether "critical" and "art" do or do not come together. It is common, now, to speak of "social practice art," but this rubric underscores how removed art is from everyday life, even as it attempts to close that divide. In fact, rather than hold the two terms together, such rubrics tend to release a given practice from the criteria of either social effectivity or artistic invention; the one tends to become the alibi for the other. Any pressure from the one side is dismissed as sociological: if you think of your concern as art in the question of social effectivity you bracket art. And any pressure from the other side can be dismissed as aestheticist: you think that you're really involved in social practice, but why should you attend to criteria of artistic convention? So the announced resolution of the two breaks down once again.

Let me end with an opposition that, though schematic, seems pertinent to this predicament — for me, this captures a lot about our moment, at least in art ...

Opposition

On the one side, there is the quasi-Gramscian position of activist art that, with aesthetic autonomy dispatched by an unholy alliance of critique and capital, sees a field wide open for social practice.

On the other side, there is the quasi-Adornian position that insists on the category of art, but with the forlorn sense that its minimal autonomy now holds minimal negativity, with nothing left to do but go through the formalist motions.

Our situation evokes the 1920s in alarming ways: economically as an age of boom and bust; politically as a period in which a state of emergency becomes more normal than exceptional; and artistically as a time when, as some practitioners act out economic crisis and political emergency as the Dadaists did, or build from this chaos as the Constructivists did, others flee it in a return to order. If there is anything to this echo it is a bad time to go post-critical.

Facticity

Neil Denari

Exploit

The premise of the day is fantastic — it made me think a lot about how we work. I had to examine the aims of our office and I pulled out an old term — "facticity" — that I'm sure, after I get through with this, you're going to use, and it's going to be cool again. It's a two hundred-and-twenty year old word, first used by Johann Fichte, Kant's younger contemporary. It's a term that fits perfectly with how we approach our work.

Facticity is both a limitation and a condition of freedom. It's a term that's so open ended and ambiguous that it allows you to state an architectural project of precision, of material fact- ness, of response to program, and so forth, without the duress of dogma. It allows the open-endedness of freedoms that we ourselves establish. Exploiting freedoms is a way to make sure those same freedoms don't become pedantic ideas.

Problems

There are two kinds of problems: One is the functional problem — things that require solutions. We know we can solve these problems. Functional problems are things culture agrees on, such as housing the homeless, or making sustainable buildings. We agree those are good issues that need to be addressed. They're our version of medicine; they need to be fixed.

And then there are disciplinary problems, which we call obsessions and Hal might call fetishes. Obsessions explore territory for which there is little use value, especially compared to the first type of problem. Obsessions find solutions to problems that don't exist. I'm going to offer a logic for why architects invent problems in the face of the dramatic complexity with which architecture is always presented.

Obsession

We have an obsession with the shaped canvas. In the 1960s a number of artists explored the geometric manipulation of the canvas perimeter. Culture didn't ask artists to reshape canvasses in the 1960s. Artists operating in a mode of crisis about where painting would go disfigured the perimeter of the canvas so the traditional pictorial nature of painting would disappear. In the work of Frank Stella, which we know as the ultimate "what you see is what you see" painting, the offset lines dramatize the shape of the canvas. We know shaped canvasses lasted for five or six years and then it was over. That says something curious about the shelf life of ideas that attempt to critique paradigms.

Culture didn't ask for these solutions. These artists invented the problem and made a proposition.

Gratuitous

Here's a quote from Jean Baudrillard's The System of Objects, *a discussion of consumer culture, advertising, and the rise of technology in the sixties: "Automatism per se is simply a technical deviation, but it opens the door to a whole world of functional delusion, to the entire range of manufactured objects in which a role is played by irrational complexity, obsessive detail, eccentric technicity, or gratuitous formalism."*

Now, when I read that — and I've read it over and over again — I have to ask myself, "Is that what I do?"

I guess it is.

Architect

The three projects I'm going to show all have to do with shaped windows. I want you to keep the shaped canvas in mind, because culture didn't ask for these windows, nor did the clients. The architects asked for these windows.

Excess

Problem number one: The Russian middle class and its new identity. Could there be an aesthetic that's indifferent to class? The client was the son of billionaire St. Petersburg bankers who had decided to put money into developing a new city for about 100,000 people.

So, straight away, you're trying to take on the issue of diversity.

We said, "No rectangular windows. We'll do anything but make rectangular windows." The grid, as it was built, not only in Soviet-era housing, but all over the place, was a sign of efficiency and nothing more. The grid was a solution to a problem that had no imaginary in it.

We sought excess.

Appearance

Problem number two: A world for a family of four. The client said: "We like modern architecture, but we don't like all the glass. We like the Case Study houses and we would hire Ray Kappe, the great modern master, to design it, but we don't want it to feel too open." The typical client in California usually says he wants to live outside and wants a glass pavilion. That represents the greatest sense of optimism, care, and curiosity about modern architecture. This family was different; they wanted mass, surface, and enclosure, at the same time as it had a sense of openness and connectivity.

The problem in this project centers on mass without massiveness: how to make a house open yet private?

We had to develop a project that was about an appearance of mass. We shaped the windows in a deeply three-dimensional way.

Curiosity

Problem number three: How to stand out and fit in at the same time? The project is on the High Line, a building that is larger than the site would allow.

It's either a serious piece of architecture or a weird curiosity — an aberrant building that is nothing more than a folly. You can decide for yourself.

On the glass façade there is a ceramic frit corresponding to the shape of the eight-inch steel pipe columns coated with intumescent paint behind the glass. If you're going to make a project that is aberrant and sort of strange, the least you can do is explain what's going on. And the only way to explain what's going on is, on the one hand, to explain through the profile that the building doesn't fit the site, and, on the other, to show that in order to be able to build that profile you need to structure it in a particular way.

Budget

One might ask: Why on earth would you put the detail on the glass? Why would you bother with that? In fact, at one point, our client, after looking at it for so long, and given the $200,000 cost of the frit, suggested taking it off to save money. We did renderings without it. Our client, who might be an aficionado of architecture, but is definitely not an architect, said, "Oh, I get it; put it back on."

Trained Judgment

Ben van Berkel

Expansion

I'd like to discuss the topic of trained judgment. Architects are dealing with an enormous expansion of the profession today. A century ago, we talked about functionality as a topic that stood on its own. Now we deal with countless efficiencies, regulations, and complex knowledge types, all requiring their own complement of specialists. The beauty of contemporary practice is that we can't separate these strands as we once did. There was a time when we thought more singularly about the modern project. Today we put these different aspects of architecture into a circle — even, sometimes, a twisted circle — and it is becoming ever more difficult to identify what is active in any given project.

Science

Architects are like scientists. We have to deal with our personal biases — the interpretive "I." We make choices. At the same time, we gain knowledge through the way we produce, which in turn forms our engagement with the public.

Architectural knowledge is advanced by the way we develop this subjectivity. How we receive our work, how we learn from it, and how we produce results is an empirical negotiation. Sometimes, in the process of design, we come into an oceanic feeling, lost among the innumerable qualities, revelations, and topics we have to deal with. On the other hand, it is helpful to go back to what was called, in the last century, "operative" criticality. What do we do with the instrument of architecture? What is the apparatus of architecture? How can we make it newly objective? What is our status as trained experts?

See

*We often explore the role of a subset of architecture —
an instrument or prototype, like a pavilion — that can be
transported into other projects. The foyer in a theater, for
example, is a vertical space from which you constantly
have vistas and see the public moving among the different
realities of the building. In some of our prototypes we've been
exploring a form of parallax: a perspective in which the view
is not just in front of you, but is also behind you, under you, or
above you. The views can be kaleidoscopic. In the exhibition
we installed at Harvard last year, we projected images across
different walls, giving the sense that you could step into
other spaces. Sometimes you wouldn't know if a person was
real or not. Were they another exhibition viewer or someone
appearing in the projected image? We discovered that it is not
the image that is most important, but the after-image. Only
after you stand back from the object do you discover what the
object was all about.*

Kaleidoscope

The twist in our work, which often constructs a public moment, is both physical and metaphorical. One has the sense that spaces are following you ... a kaleidoscopic relationship between space and time. You can ramp down in one spiral, combine it with another spiral, and go on to yet another. There's always another possible step. You are walking within one space-time and simultaneously seeing into another.

Reference

It isn't necessary to make buildings refer to their program. It could be a museum, it could be a department store, it could be an electricity station, and it could be an artwork. A public building is a lamp within the city, not a functional symbol.

Future

I think it's impossible to make an architecture that is future-oriented.

Invisible

In the central atrium of the Mercedes-Benz Museum we installed a tornado-inducing device that sucks out smoke from the building during a fire. This allowed us to create a totally open building. The invisible invention of a couple of engineers and ourselves allowed us to design a building with no compartmentalization, reducing an enormous amount of material and a great amount of cost. This highly technological innovation gave me an insight into how we can rethink architecture through scientific innovation.

Combine

We often work with people outside of architecture to inform our knowledge. If design is subjective and construction is objective, I would argue that architecture is what Lorraine Daston and Peter Galison call "trained judgment." We have to know how to combine information. Objectivity is not a phenomenon wherein we don't make choices.

Care

Who cares about the box or the blob?

Work

This brings me to the notion of criticality. Criticality is only compelling when we make it operative, when we make it instrumental, when it helps us select information in order to make the project work.

Technique

It's not about design techniques. It is about what design techniques can do.

The Nightmare
of Participation

Markus Miessen

Gap

I've been introduced as a writer, but I also work as an architect and consultant. I work between two kinds of structures: one is called Studio Miessen and the other is a purely individual practice. There's a clear separation. Everything that happens in my individual practice — research, writing, teaching, and consulting — is non-physical and any spatial or physical commissions are dealt through Studio Miessen, which is an architectural practice in the sense that it deals with physical "stuff."

Romantic

I've been working on the issue of participation since 2004. Of course, since the mid-nineties, in the arts and in architecture, participation has been highly romanticized; but this romantic view falls far short of what participation could possibly be and contribute.

In 2004, I began wondering whether we really mean "participate," or whether we mean something else. In the early 2000s, as Tony Blair's New Labor tried to implement more and more consensual participatory structures, the willingness of the general public to participate in those structures decreased. Participation was being used as a tool for political legitimatization. It was not a bottom-up endeavor, but one in which a hierarchical structure says, "We've given you the space of participation. If you haven't participated, that's your problem. We're immune from judgment or critique."

Wedge

I've become interested in a type of participation that forces entry into a field or area of knowledge where you're usually not welcome and where your background is not necessarily deemed relevant. This is a practice without mandate or commission. It is not a practice where someone asks you to do something.

Participation, in this model, is self-initiated by an individual or a collective trying to enter an off-limits discussion. This is what I would call critical spatial practice. This is not a term that I'm introducing. It's a term that has been around for some time.

Meddling

If the model of participation as consensus amounts to a withdrawal of responsibility, my question would be: How can one assume a certain responsibility within one's own practice?

When we talk about participation in architecture we often talk about participation in the sense of social work or doing good. I would like to challenge this and ask: What does it really mean to assume agency? Who are you talking to? Which position are you talking from?

There's a German word — "Einmischung" — that means "meddling": insisting on getting involved.

Irritation

In looking back at the last fifteen years and to the future, I'm continually asking: How has the role of the architect changed? How can the architect's role be redefined given changing aspects of contemporary practice — for example, the different fields or backgrounds one has to assume in certain projects: designing, inserting, instigating, conducting, mediating, curating, the role of the politician, etc.? How could there be a productive relationship between enabling — which architects are good at — and irritation? How can irritation become productive?

Nasty

We invited fifty people from around the world — curators, politicians, writers, poets, architects, artists — to contribute to the Lyon Biennale by sending us a visualization of their spatial perception of Europe; they could draw, take a photograph, write something, ...

We designed this nasty looking table: a space of dissensus, where no conversation takes place — no negotiation; you are in a setting that is more like an election booth.

We hung the representations of Europe on the back wall and photocopies of these representations were placed in the middle of the table; the only shared space.

The Biennale audience was asked to take those representations and superimpose their own spatial perceptions of Europe — to hijack and corrupt.

Export

There was an interesting moment, post-9/11, when universities (especially American) decided to start satellite campuses in the Middle East. Universities built campuses and professors would fly in for three years, with no previous experience in the region and no local knowledge. They would teach the same curriculum that they would have been teaching in the US. Then they would leave and someone else would come.

In 2007 I started — in collaboration with the Architectural Association — a small program in the Emirates, originally in Dubai.

I would bring in people from all over the world to collaborate with the locals. The participants — local and international teachers and students — were always organized into teams.

There would always be a shared space of thought and production.

Altruism

For various reasons, I broke the relationship with the AA. Partly, this decision concerned the issue of fees.

I started a non-profit organization.

Self-Awareness

You need the critical awareness to look at what's happening in your own backyard before you claim things about other conditions. The central focus of the workshops was to begin a dialogue about productive alternatives.

In the first year of the Dubai initiative, the students looked specifically at labor conditions. They organized conversations and interviews with people across the social spectrum of Dubai — a Bangladeshi construction worker; a Russian prostitute; a South Korean mobile phone dealer; a European investment banker; a German cultural attaché; ... All of these people share a single attribute: everyone in Dubai is on three-year contracts. At that time there were 1.3 million people living in Dubai, of which only 35,000 were Emiratis. Anyone on a temporary contract can be thrown out of the country at any point in time.

JUDGMENT

Conversation I

Ben van Berkel, Neil Denari, Hal Foster, Markus Miessen, Sarah Whiting

Grant Alford, Giorgio Angelini, Graham Bader, Scott Colman,
Christopher Hight, Gordon Hughes, Carlos Jiménez, Albert Pope,
Bryony Roberts, among others.

Sarah Whiting: The intention of this symposium is to bring together critical judgment and operative judgment — to see where they intersect. I'd like to highlight a simple framework in which criticism and production are inseparably connected. And I'd like to contrast this framework with another that has typified thinking in recent years, namely that criticism and production have each served as the other's straw-man.

Hal Foster: I was struck by our generational differences in presentation, but I think we agree on the value of intervention. Markus, you're skeptical of the political uses of participation, but isn't your critique of participation culturally specific and maybe European specific? For example, when French theory, as we used to call it, came to the United States, with its fundamental call for decentering, its cultural specificity was lost. France is centered — intellectually, politically, and administratively — in ways in which the United States is not. So I wonder if your critique of participation might have a different valence where political participation runs at well under fifty percent and the problem is not consensus but a reflexive and rigid agonism? It's obvious that what we have is not the dissensus that you and Chantal Mouffe have in mind.

Markus Miessen: It's striking today that the discourse around social networks is led as if it were a movement. It's very different from a social movement.

Foster: I tend to agree with you in terms of social movements. But what about Occupy Wall Street, which is, if not an architectural practice, certainly a spatial practice? It's precisely not about a set of positions; they refuse organization. I tend to think politics without a position is not politics. In the different versions of Occupy Wall Street around the country, any institution in power consistently refuses to take it up as a movement. Yet it seems to be a success so far. It's not just "check this box if you hate that senator." It seems to use social media in a way that has begun to have political reflexivity. I wonder how that fits into your genealogy?

Miessen: Maybe it's less easily dismissible because it spatializes. A lot of the things online are interesting, but the spatial is still super important. I'm not just saying this because I have an architecture background. As soon as something spatializes, it creates a completely different reality. I'm not interested in the passive idea of participation: "join." I'm interested in an active engagement, in which an individual or collective starts something.

Giorgio Angelini: Isn't Occupy Wall Street, in its resistance to being co-opted and its departure from older definitions of resistance, the embodiment of post-criticality?

Foster: I don't see it as post-critical. Its critique is evident. It just refuses to specify all its terms right now. It's a critique in formation. It also resists the usual argument that politics and social media don't need actual space.

Angelini: As soon as it defines itself and takes a specific position, will it lose the attributes you find so laudable?

Foster: Yes, but not the slogan attached to it: "We are the ninety-nine percent." It's important to keep the space of the ninety-nine percent open as long as possible.

Whiting: I think it's important to figure out whether that's a deliberate attempt to keep things open or an inability to coalesce.

Foster: It's not an inability to coalesce. They've been there every day for a month in Manhattan. Saturday is going to be a big day in many cities.

Graham Bader: It's a deliberate effort not to lay out a specific critical position and therefore take an enlightened position. Something very interesting is occurring when people are fully aware of maintaining a position, yet don't want their specific demands co-opted. It's very relevant to the topic of judgment we're discussing.

Foster: The platform hasn't coalesced. Marx said — to quote the bible — any revolutionary group in formation doesn't really know what it wants. That's what makes the revolution. It wants an alternative. That, to me, is where critique is absolutely essential. There are no alternatives for that critique. Yet, many people think it shuts down alternatives.

Bader: I'm not disagreeing. What makes Occupy Wall Street very interesting is that you have a battle over what this means front and center in the public discussion and that makes it more potent.

Whiting: You ended your presentation, Hal, with a parallel between today and the 1920s. There is an implication that you would advocate we not fall into the thirties. What's the way out? Or are you closing the door to a way out?

Foster: This is where I take the critique of critical authority to heart. It's not really critical to propose a way out. That's the interest of the political movements you've witnessed over the last nine months or so. If you saw these protests in the last month it seems to be the real deal — the last month has turned more dangerous. I don't have any platform or prospect.

Whiting: In your architectural criticism, I admire your willingness to deal with a wide range of topics, ranging from more avant-garde figures — or those who assume the position of the avant-garde, like Zaha Hadid or Diller Scofidio Renfro — to more normative practices. You're trying to understand the position of things that get built and their built effects. But if you take the position that the critic is not able to help point the way out of a crisis, I wonder if that's disingenuous given the criticism you publish. Your public voice is different from the more academic voice we heard this morning. I fully agree with your plea for the continued relevance and significance of criticism and judgment, but I was stymied by the closed-door at the end of your presentation. What is the relationship between the platform you laid out — opening the question of relevance, making a plea for relevance, and then essentially dismantling much contemporary theory in light of that desire for relevance — and where you left us? In terms of the academy, where do you allow possibilities for, let's say, reintroducing the criticism and judgment that you feel are so important?

Foster: I'm stymied by your question. I don't feel that I ended with a dead end. I ended with an historical caution, that's all. Let me answer in reverse. This is not merely anecdotal: For people of my generation, formed in the 1970s, critical theory was the liveliest practice in the culture — art, writing, film, anything. It had an enormous presence in the academy from that point on. We were sought after and that's how I snuck into the academy. There was a real interest, a real demand, and I just don't think that's the case anymore. Like so much discourse over the last fifteen or twenty years, whole terms and languages were subtly and not-so-subtly displaced, even the innocuous idea that critical consciousness is important to a democratic citizen. That's how the humanities were advocated in the American university, but that's now become a radical thing to say. The President of Princeton is a person you and I both like and admire, but she will say things — mostly to alumni, but sometimes the faculty hears it too — like: "The scientists do truth, and you people in the humanities do passion." There's already a discourse of affect that has come to the fore. I don't mean to oppose the humanities and the sciences, but the great new paradigm is neuroscience. And that effectively does away with not only judgment but also interpretation. To advocate for critical practice and modes of evaluation and judgment seems crucial. Part of critical theory was a critique of judgment, although, not in the Kantian sense. When Kant says "critique of judgment," he means the analysis of judgment, not critique in our sense. But one could map a certain history from the critical to the affective, from truth and its complication to "you do passion."

Whiting: I don't disagree with your diagnosis. But, given that situation, how would you advocate reanimating critical inquiry within the academy? Would you advocate going back to a model, thinking it can be repositioned, or does that model require a new formulation? I'm aware that you're not going to say the critic's role is to offer new directions. But that is a professor's role. How do you position yourself within the academy?

Foster: Well, that might be the difference between an architecture school and other aspects of a university. A very simple way to think about a college or university is that its role concerns the invention of new ideas, but its role also concerns the transmission of old ones. As you know, my generation and subsequent ones were formed by a rhetoric of rupture and much of my criticism derives from two models that are about rupture. One is the neo-avant-garde and one is postmodernism. I'm now much more interested in questions of persistence and afterlife. Aby Warburg is more important to me now than Jacques Derrida. But they don't necessarily have to be opposed either. There are other ways to think about it. Too many of us, for too long, were avant-gardists of one stripe or another. I'm not interested in innovation for its own sake. But I take your point that my program, if there is a program, is not simply to revive critique as demystification. You have to take into account all the critiques of such critique, but I'm not overly impressed by the other models out there.

Gordon Hughes: It seems important to differentiate affect theory and phenomenology. With affect theory, affect is deemed *a priori* to meaning, which no phenomenologist would accept. Once meaning is bracketed out, you can't have a discussion about judgment; you respond on a purely autonomic level. That's crucial to the post-critical model that you're talking about.

Foster: We don't disagree. What we used to call phenomenological is now somehow considered affective, and they're very, very different, precisely as you described. But affect often goes under the cover of phenomenology. Ólafur Elíasson will tell you his work is about the recovery of your own perceptual apparatus. That's what phenomenology wanted with its famous bracketing. This is to demonize it too much, but there is a way in which the affective is ideological and pervasive: It's emotion that seems to be yours, but it's not really. It's the "invasion of the emotion snatchers." It comes from somewhere else. It's so internal to your feelings and emotions that it directs you. I don't mean to turn affect into the bogeyman of the present. Of course one wants an aesthetic dimension and an emotive response to architecture. Affect, for me, just has a different charge.

Whiting: In both your approaches, Neil and Ben, there is an attention to a public reading of the project, understanding that this is different from the architect's project, and an acknowledgment that the public may not necessarily be on the same plane with you. Your distinction, Neil, between problem solving and obsession was very helpful in that sense. But to what extent are you spelling out that reading of the project? I think there is a very big difference with your mapping out the structure in HL23 and Ben's obfuscating the reading of the Star Place Department Store. In the department store, if the public doesn't know what it is, that's okay. The twist multiplies the interior so there's a complexity that is difficult to read. Unlike Neil, Ben, you aren't mapping out what the public sees.

Neil Denari: I was thinking about Hal's comments on affect: it could get to the point where the possibility of having your own emotions is stolen, because those emotions are dictated to you. Ben's project could be presented as the sum total or gestalt of some mysterious, but productive, relationship between the "I" and data, whereas the frit on HL23 was obviously not dictated by either one. It wasn't the "I" that said we need to put that there. It was the curious sense of making a form of public communication for something that I knew wouldn't be explicit. I wouldn't want to have a project dictate or steal the possibility of newness, mystery, and surprise. You can come at this from a number of different directions. Even if you solve problems in ways that, behind the scenes, are super objective, they can reach a level of mystery in terms of communication.

Ben van Berkel: It's interesting that you call it mystery. Almost eighty percent of the cost of the Erasmus Bridge was public money. I had a lot of convincing to do, in order to design that bridge. But, in my mind, the project concerned more than this public interest alone. I was fascinated by the possibility that this bridge could become not a symbol or an icon but an image that would generate constructive layers of reading. Our projects often refer to their "context," or their interpretation of "context." I think it's fascinating that you can transport and instrumentalize external information through the internal aspects of architecture. When we talk about design techniques it often sounds like we're solely concerned with the instruments of design. But this is the way we communicate and I've often said, if there is no communication between the public and our work, then there's no architecture. The most recent work tries to use the abstract knowledge behind the image to generate more than one reading. In that sense, art is often much more innovative than architecture, constantly renewing its techniques, and often finding new ways, through those techniques, to convey a cultural message that is highly political or social. Architects don't often talk about what kind of culture we produce. You can't constantly think about this question of culture; but I would like to say we produce culture.

Whiting: For you, Ben, the issue of trained judgment is less about training the audience than training the architect. It's a very specific notion of training, which, in the context of judgment, is very different from Neil, who lays out an approach that is not a trained form of science or learning, but really training or honing obsession.

Denari: When you think about the difference between an artist and an architect — the architect deals with clients and cities and so forth by definition — the conventional logic would default to the service nature of architecture and say, "obsessions have nothing to do with service; they're only going to get in the way, cost more, and obfuscate." Suspicion of a project's beauty or affect aggregates responsibility to argue it's all *a priori*. I'm not for that. I'm for giving critics plenty of ammunition; for taking your obsessions into the public realm and going on record by trying to explain without killing the mystery. By "mystery" I mean a productive paradigm; something that's open ended and, to a certain extent, tries to create an exchange value for what might be private. Saying "I've worked for years on a project and I own it; the last thing I have to do is explain it to people; you either like it or you don't," is totally uninteresting to me. The work is debated, hopefully, rather than just being accepted or rejected as good, or beautiful, or a paradigm for culture. Architecture is too complicated to be reduced to that.

Albert Pope: Neil, in the end of your presentation you cast the indifference of the spectators against the effort you made to telegraph the structure of HL23 through the frit. It struck me that some of your work — unlike that building, and much like Ben's — creates a gestalt. For example, you don't express the earthquake reinforcement in the corner of the No Mass House. In most of your projects there's the intent to integrate the components. But in HL23 you don't resolve the technical issues in the way you did with the house. You play off the difference between the technical aspect, which is the structure, and the representative aspect, which is the frit. The difference between the two is the didactic moment that you discussed. The people on the High Line see that and could be confused by it, interested by it, or ignore it; but you give them an opening. There's an absence of gestalt. The technical is not reconciled to the expressive or the representational; there's a gap between them, which is that opening you were just referring to.

Denari: "Facticity" is such a pliable term because it refers to the process of saying, "Here's what it's made of; here's how we made it; here's what we went through; here's how we engineered it." I could spend an hour to take you through the logic of a building's production and the choices we made about the design. To get HL23 through city planning and have it accepted required eight exceptions to the zoning. Although the process through which it was welcomed was enigmatic, I don't want to arrest or paralyze readings and proclaim and fix. I want to embrace the curious vibration between the real and the virtual. If you're a lay person, you might say, "What is it?" If you're an architect, you might say, "That's dishonest," or, "I would never do that," or, "Wow! I didn't think of that." That's obviously the level of vibration you want in the work. In the house, where we hid the steel, the project of revealing structure wasn't the agenda. The agenda concerned mass. So every project takes on a mind of its own, even though there are parallel discourses. The task is to make arguments that are mysterious at one level and reasonable at another level. Facticity allows freedom, particularly if you're obsessed, like we are, about making sure that our buildings are built exactly the way we want them to be built. For many that's not a radical project. But, if you build something precise, you won't notice that it is. Architects always notice when things aren't built well. But when it's built well, you don't look for the mistakes; you accept the arguments. It's a conduit for explaining, but, obviously, not in a hammering way. That's why I can have an obsession for finish, but not have it be an endgame.

Whiting: I want to ask each of you to address the role of judgment within the university, and specifically within a school of architecture, vis-à-vis your respective platforms.

Denari: "Resistance" was such a strong wash-word in *The Anti-Aesthetic*, especially with Kenneth Frampton and Jean Baudrillard. Given commercial pressures today, it's important to think about practice in the realm of persistence or even acceptance. In school, we're not telling students, "You're in the wrong place. You should quit." The best project is one that continues to resist and question the nature of how you practice to create effects, beyond the traditional ways of getting a commission and building a project. That question is very important today: How do you practice with so many forces and conditions working against you?

For me, it's important that a school be diverse rather than homogeneous. You're not going to find out how a project or an agenda becomes useful or critical when it's taught as brainwashing or hyper-technique. The extent to which everybody's willing to fess-up and make his or her argument part of a conversation is the only way in which anything becomes interesting. It opposes the vocational project of teaching something that in five years a student won't use anymore. The vitality of schools and teaching are about that and that's what we're doing here today.

Grant Alford: In your work, Ben, it seems you believe culture is technologically driven and as an architect you acknowledge and engage that. You arrive at the forms and the kind of practice you have through a technological production. Neil, you don't talk about technology as much. It seems your practice is driven by your obsession and then you submit the forms that you create to become the culture over time. In your practice, Ben, the architect engages a culture that's given, whereas yours, Neil, is driving culture.

Berkel: Recently, I have been saying that architects work with an orchestra of specialists where each performer plays a different instrument and sits facing a totally different direction. Working through that kind of orchestra I've discovered there is more music to be found if you go deeper and if you expand. The next generation will have a different understanding of how to transform spatial effects into digital and programming techniques than today's architects. I like your comment, because there's a lot of technological innovation in fields like product design, but in architecture we are quite behind. Trained judgment is also connected to personal experience and working, for such a long time, with contemporary methods. Of course, computation is playing an enormously important role in the field. But my thoughts have gone lately toward the questions: How did the computer really revolutionize architecture? and What could the computer do in the future? It has been too easy in the last five years. The early years were highly experimental; everything was possible and we've seen, more recently, that much was even buildable. But architecture is not dealing with how we can get optimum knowledge and intelligence out of the computational instrument. It may sound conservative, but I'm interested in a new form of discipline, in particular, how to discipline. It's possible to train architects to make better choices for how they use these instruments.

Denari: My office is much smaller than Ben's and Ben has far more projects. The way in which Ben's office has to deal with production and quantity requires a different process, but no less engagement. I have a few projects and less than ten people. I'm left to my own devices, without the provocation to extrapolate across a lot of different types of projects and expand possibilities or working methods. I'm the only one in the office who can come in with ideas, because that's the way it's set up. The work of the office tends toward the problems I introduce into the conversation. I'd love to be in Ben's situation. In the United States it's more challenging to do that. So there are immediate conditions on the table that define our respective approaches.

Pope: In the project for the European Kunsthalle in Cologne, Markus, you began with a critique of the big art institution and the Bilbao effect and suggested that all you really need to make an institution is a computer, a phone, and other technology. This may be a recipe for post-bubble architecture and it resonates with Hal's comment that affect has become pre-emptive. In many ways, affect is something aesthetically pre-digested and you can easily associate that with the excesses of institutional architecture. But, for Ben and Neil, there is friction between the technical and the affective. So we can't really say that we can reduce an institution down to a coffee machine and a computer, as attractive as that is. In the case of Cologne, you had the medieval fabric of the city to work with. There was enormous affect there. It's the necessary friction between the technical and the affective that keeps an environment from becoming aesthetically pre-digested and preemptive.

Miessen: I hope I didn't come across as taking a position against the physical. I'm also very interested in the physical. In the office we work on many projects that have some kind of physical presence. The point I want to make is that with budgetary constraints today, there is often a mismatch between architectural budgets and program budgets. One should at least consider to what extent the physical is needed or could be reduced in order to make budgetary space for other things. That sounds like I'm against architecture. Because I don't build to the extent that someone else would, my practice doesn't fit with the preconceived role of the architect. I think that's also part of education. How can you educate clients so they understand that architecture doesn't mean everything has to be physical?

Pope: Yes, but given the distinction between an architect and an event planner: as powerful as events are, they're not generally engaged with form as a specific problem. As architects we're talking about the friction between the technical and expressive means; but we're also talking about events as well.

Miessen: From my point of view, the question is whether, at the end of the day, the effect of whatever you produce is somehow spatial or can be read through something spatial and how, with an architectural background, you have a different reading of space than an event planner. But that, of course, is debatable. One might find that, after having done the project, you realize you failed completely and maybe in the next project you start to really rethink things.

Bryony Roberts: Markus, I wanted to ask you about this exchange between discourse and form making, because it points to the issue of how critique and architecture are sometimes incompatible. It's fabulous that you want to make this space for a dissensual debate and the meeting of political groups, but I'm wondering how that becomes architecture and finds form. Often the debates you stage are reflections on representations of space, or find spaces in the city that can be occupied, but it's very difficult to pin down any organizational strategy, because that limitation would counter your ambitions in some way. Do you see a way that dissensual conversation can become architectural?

Miessen: In a number of our projects we try to develop a space that becomes singular in its physicality: a space wherein a lot of different programs are overlapped. This interests us because it creates conflicts between different users and stimulates a constant negotiation between different stakeholders or groups. Of course, at the end of the day, it comes back to this question of the moment one finally makes a decision. It immediately turns into an aesthetic decision because it's physical. It would then be up to you to judge whether you find this appealing or not. It's very difficult to judge from an image, because we're interested in the way this space performs and creates conflict. In order to judge, one would have to experience it as space.

Foster: Do we just give up and become critics of spatial practice or critics of artists? The presentations of Ben and Neil this afternoon inspired me to emphatically say "No." I heard an idea of criticality reinvented. Neil, you begin on the subjective side and push towards the objective or the technical, and you, Ben, were more on the objective or technical side and look for decisions that can make those models actual. This whole resolution of the objective and the subjective is really the aesthetic according to Kant. That's what aesthetic judgment is. One critique of the Kantian aesthetic asserts this moment of reconciliation is always a forced consensus and not a magical resolution of a fundamental contradiction between the subjective and the objective. But in the presentations of your work, the moment where those two things are held together becomes a critical moment. In fact, Ben disclosed it as the moment of criticality, where the thing works, somehow. I think that's a profound aesthetic moment. But it's also a profound critical moment that has all kinds of cultural resonance. I could say a lot more about that, but I think that's really an argument for the expertise of a school of architecture. It's not a moment that's merely conciliatory or consensual.

Stella's shaped canvases are, to use a term of Michael Fried, "deductive structures." They seem absolutely motivated, such that everything is determined by the shape. That's absolutely objective. But, Stella can never get rid of the first moment of choice, which is not only subjective but also arbitrary. Stella holds together the arbitrary and the motivated in a very intense way, and, in a certain way, Neil does too, with his arbitrary choice of the shaped window. But once that shaped window is worked out — scenographically, structurally, spatially, and programmatically — it becomes objective. Ben does the same thing, but from the other direction, it seems to me. And I think that's the moment where the public says, "Yes! I get it!" It's not a moment of false reconciliation; it's a moment of critical consciousness.

Denari: A student is always looking for the most amount of common sense to be able to leverage the work, so choice is deferred because choice is scary. Design hinges on the arbitrary and the only way that you can leverage the arbitrary is to have a few years on you and be able to risk it. Then, even if you reverse engineer it, that's part of the process. Common sense then comes to mean collective agreement. So, when somebody says, "That works," another hears, "That works; it's the most amount of applied common sense." It's a critical moment when that occurs. When there is no axiom of common sense, it's either beyond plausible or persuasive, in which case it becomes an accumulation of common energy. For me, when a building reaches its apex, it works across a series of levels from the pragmatic to the emotional. None is good enough. It's the agent of compromise or conciliation, but I don't look at it as negative. It's a zenith coming together. That's the aspiration for the work.

Roberts: Hal, your point seems very different from the critical project you were initially describing or that I would characterize as critical theory, which fundamentally questions modes of production or economic and political power structures. Although I think it's important to acknowledge that critical theory is waning, the challenge is and has always been that, in searching for alternatives, it's very difficult to actually build something, because you end up committing to a certain system of economic power or permanence when you make a commitment to form. This is always the apprehension and it points to the tension between events and architecture that came up earlier. I was surprised to hear you argue new possibilities for the critical in work that is so vehemently architectural and in work aligned with late capitalism: aspects

69

that would have been very problematic for earlier critical positions.

Foster: Yes, sure. Can't there be more than one critical position? A critic — and this is true of most artists too — is intrinsically critical in their disposition. There's a freedom in the semi-autonomy of art and criticism that's paid for by a relative lack of intervention and effectivity. I don't think there's just one critical attitude. But there's a difference between a moment of critical consciousness that might be a public moment, or a quasi-public moment, and an idea of common sense. The idea of the commons is very much with us, and I think it's extremely important right now, for all kinds of reasons — ecologically, politically, etc. But one of the great targets of criticism is common sense. There's a great line in Sartre, where he talks about the commonplace as the most hackneyed of things, but it's also the most communal of things. Sartre says, "the commonplace belongs to everybody; it is the presence of everybody in me." When I utter a cliché, no one owns it. I think the common is a very complicated question right now.

Whiting: There is a distinction between common sense in terms of pragmatism and the *sensus communis* as a wave of agreement or tie among us.

Foster: If critical theory is at all for you a suspicion of humanism, then *sensus communis* is a difficult term. Kant proposed an idea of universal humanness. For generations of critical theorists that's still a very tricky opposition.

Christopher Hight: With Kant and the universality of the humanist position, the possibility of critique depended on the existence of the transcendental *a priori*. As that project advanced and became the subject of the critical project — in Foucault for example — the transcendental *a priori* became the historical *a priori*, more immanent to the constructions of culture. It struck me that, in many ways, both Ben and Neil are struggling for, with, or around, the reverse of those relationships. With the historical *a priori* and an immanent material condition through which you make judgments and critical evaluations, the question was always: What are the conditions of possibility for a certain kind of formation, for a certain kind of order, for a certain kind of stability, or an organization of culture? The earlier comments reverse that to ask: What are the possibilities for other conditions? Whether you take an obsession, or start with a series of techniques, you use those techniques as a series of estranging strategies, different than how you've previously used techniques, to manifest a building. Architecture is always opening a passage to other conditions and leaving that space open without entirely giving finality to that answer. That may be the possibility of a different kind of critique within architecture, that's projective but nevertheless not synthetic.

Scott Colman: In the academy we should definitely be making students conscious of the techniques of the field. I'm not sure that's what we should be doing in public though. We need to be really clear about which audience we're talking about. And if we just take a position that we need to be critical because we can open up the field, then it's too passive and, frankly, uncritical for me.

Berkel: A scientist would not explain the techniques of science to the public. But when it comes to urban planning, I'm often surprised when I explain certain aspects of how the city operates. Today the city, especially in America, is so decentralized — politically, and in terms of circulation —

that cities become self-supportive. Cities need to be brands today. You need to promote your city otherwise everything goes away. Often politicians don't know how to explain their cities or understand how they really operate physically — for example: Why do people leave? How do certain behaviors migrate? With respect to urban questions, architects are secluding themselves too much. A politician needs to talk to the public every day. We talk to the public maybe once every three months. How do we make instruments that help the city become clearer to the public? You may have heard me talk about deep planning, which is an attempt to find new means to present certain information about aspects of the city. These digital visualization techniques gave us an incredible new form of insight and allowed us to set up a dialogue with the public and the politicians to rethink the city. So I think it's right that, as architects, we don't need to communicate our techniques to the public, but for urban planning, I would argue, it's the other way around.

Whiting: Ben, you've constantly underscored the expansion of our discipline in terms of practice and expertise. You've profited from that expansion. For example, the fire solution in the Benz Museum enabled you to do a building that didn't have compartments and that allowed a different kind of architecture. Is it possible to bring that expertise into the academy without pushing out some of the questions of our own field, like the obsessions that interest Neil? Do you expand architectural education to more years? Do you create tracks of specialties? I'm intrigued that your response to Scott only talked about the public side as opposed to talking about the academic side.

Berkel: That's why I teach at the Städelschule. The Städelschule sets up a totally different dialogue with artists, philosophers, and others in the university beyond the profession of architecture. This breadth is an important part of education that, we all know, needs stimulation. Of course, one also needs to stimulate the imagination and open up the eye of the student. But that's only one side. For that reason, I talked about the scientific self, which concerns this notion of common sense. How can we talk in architectural education about common sense? I think it's very hard. In my opinion, it's very important to promote originality. And originality only comes from research and experimentation. But, if you don't know what you're resources are and your own specialties, you can't have a dialogue with others. So I think we should try much harder to expand the academic dialogue, beyond the purely artistic aspects of what we produce, beyond what we call originality in architecture. I believe the scientific aspect of the profession has expanded so wildly that we have lost our grasp on that aspect. We must train ourselves to deal with these instruments by teaching a more holistic approach. Universities were segmented in the sixties and seventies. We should try hard to bring that knowledge back into the profession.

Denari: I think it's a curious moment where technique as content — "I have this tool, I can do this." — is essentially being replaced by "What will I do with it?" If there's anything lingering in schools, it's the idea of technique as content. In Ben's or my process, there's no value in technique as content. We get no credit for saying we can communicate digitally. I constantly tell my students: "So what if you know how to make a rendering. I don't care. We need to talk about the proposition." It's wrong to believe digital tools will automatically allow everybody to make precise things as though the digital produces projects *a priori*. I don't have that view because I was trained to draw by hand and feel there's a kinesthetic loss in using computers. The digital allows a different kind of facility, which, in many ways, is trainable, but is also based on a curious form of talent. We're looking for ways in which talent gets transposed through different tools. Eyes are still eyes. Computers set up global generics and one must work very hard to resist those things. Ben uses the term "misuse" and I have always liked the idea of productive misuse. Brian Eno, the musician, always threw away the handbook when he got a new keyboard. He wanted to use it incorrectly, to generate new things. But the computer can obviously become problematic, if you don't know how to rework or rethink it and, based on your agenda, change software to be more operative and proprietary for you. In parametric design, you have to know more up-front about what you want to do, as opposed to "close your eyes" and hope that it will give you something. I think there's a mythology of closing the eyes in our generation. An older generation knew there was rigorous thinking that's *a priori*. It's not pre-figuring, or creating an image and then using the tool to build it, but neither is it a device that, through data, or through the operativity of the software, will give you something automatically, although there's a large group of people who believe that. I don't have an evangelical sense of what the digital is about. So caution is probably reasonable in any medium. And I don't think it means there are amateurs and experts, because I champion the amateur. Once you become an expert, you're dead; you just keep doing the same thing. It's easy to see that there are digital aesthetics out there, but I would say our work is not a digital aesthetic, even though, of course, in today's world, we engage specialists and trade information across continents.

Berkel: I agree. In my work, the use of digital technology is heavily celebrated, although it's more about how we edit and filter information. I'm highly critical of attempts to use the computer to generate the most interesting, reductive, or highly complex forms alone. After the diagram, we entered a phase in which we now work on the principle of the design model — thought models, you could say — in which you begin to design the way you gain knowledge. Editing, like writing, is a constant process. For that reason, the computational can be a very hermetic science in our field. Lately, I have been talking about the intelligence of the computational instead of the formal, because the formal has been exploited for more than ten years now. The formal is not the most interesting future of the computational; it's the informational. How can you rethink and proportion information? We have a long history of proportioning buildings, so why not use that history in a new way to gain control over new parts of the discipline? We need to rethink new forms — new concepts — of control. That doesn't mean control in the heavy sense, but how you juggle the pieces and gather information.

Miessen: At the end of the day the question is: "What do we really add to the conversation?" For the general public, it's quite difficult to understand what an architect can add. Ben and Neil's practices are brilliant examples of what architecture can add, but we have to be honest that the kind of architecture we're talking about in this room is less than one percent of the architecture out there. It would be interesting to really question how one could change the reception of architecture, particularly the changing role of architecture in the current economic climate. I don't want to be a pessimist, but I don't think the economics will change for two decades or so.

Whiting: The indeterminate and often fleeting projects that you talked about in your series of examples, Markus, form a practice in which time is part of your material; events structure possible moments of practice. This is an interesting contrast to the architects in the symposium who necessarily have, through the obligation of architecture, more form-based and slower practices. I wonder how your practice fits into the rapid and dense categorization that Hal offered us, in terms of a mode of practice that maintains a form of criticality, but pushes forward?

Miessen: The way we practice challenges the status quo. Whether we call this critical doesn't really matter. Questioning the romantic model of participation doesn't devalue the efforts of people who work within participatory practices. Participation can be incredibly enriching. Something like Architecture for Humanity is a great project, but lacks criticality insofar as it takes for granted a certain idea of practice: it's architecture as a service — spatial provision that assumes the person you're building for is somehow different than you. We also talk about the public as if there was one public, but, of course, in the contexts in which we operate, there are very different publics, and they exist on very different scales. We don't like to talk about the fact that within public buildings we're invariably involved in some form of social engineering. We are creating the public that is then invited to be involved in or become activists within those buildings. This will become increasingly relevant: How does one create those publics in order to create a dissensual forum? By creating certain conflicts or problems, you can widen the scope of those institutions. This concerns the issue of problem solving: one encounters certain problems or one comes up with problems and then tries to solve them. But I'm wondering whether problems always need to be solved. It can also be our job to create certain problems, in order for those problems to stimulate something else.

Whiting: There's a language of dissent in your statements Markus, which evolves out of Chantal Mouffe and the idea of provocation. I have some issue with dissent being automatic — "Oh, it must be better to put a burr in the saddle." — as opposed to provocation, which has the possibility of tweaking or swerving and is not simply upending. I completely agree that participation can be an opiate and misused, but I'm not sure that automatically means dissent is the answer.

Miessen: I absolutely agree with you. When I call for a dissensual forum, I really mean some kind of irritation within the system that becomes productive. This comes back to Ben's point about being operative. I think that's absolutely crucial, otherwise it becomes more a hindrance than something that moves forward. I also have issues with Mouffe. She's very good at explaining a certain problem, but every time one tries to nail her down in terms of making propositions, even if they're unspecific, she wouldn't do it.

Foster: This is about problem, solution, problem, solution ... That's the story of art history and of architectural history, as told since Hegel, but both are encoded as process and Neil and Ben gave examples today whereby a project can be a solution to a problem but also problematize its own conditions. To refer back to Christopher's comments on Foucault: a solution can also lay bare what the situation is and thus be problematic in a provocative sense for other practitioners.

Carlos Jiménez: Hal, I was very taken by your fifteen-minute summation of affairs, but I was left with a very distraught feeling that critics have become completely irrelevant. Your brilliance is evident in everything that you mentioned, but it seems critics once mobilized change, and we are left with this rather pessimistic feeling that we have returned to the thirties, where the critic can no longer be a force to instigate and motivate people for change. There is a sense of resignation. I would like to challenge your brilliance to give us some hint of what the post-critical critic may be? If you take Herbert Muschamp, who was always promoting his favorite architects, we have an intermediate critic, but the latest *New York Times* critic, Michael Kimmelman, leaves the architect as the last author of architecture. The *Times* has become very critical of the way architects have been misbehaving. What are the instruments that a critic has to offer a society that has become rather forgetful and rather celebratory of, not fifteen minutes of condensed knowledge, but fifteen minutes of fame?

Foster: That's a tough one. I didn't mean to make anyone distraught, except me. Because I do think it's a dire condition. I think the old Gramscian line, "optimism of the will, pessimism of the intellect," is always a good one. I do think, objectively, that the condition of the critic is dire. The critic — the theorist — had such prestige; there was a way in which critical theory was the last great avant-garde of the twentieth century. The art critic was an important mediator between practice and the public for generations. Criticism emerged with the bourgeois public sphere and, although it had good decades and not-so-good decades, there are great and crucial figures in the past. That's not the case in the art world today. I escaped to the academy as a last-ditch resort. It was really a sanctuary, because the market closed in on criticism in the 1980s and what displaced the critic was the new importance of dealers — I refuse to call dealers "gallerists" — collectors, and curators. In part it was our own fault, because even though I'm nostalgic for the heyday of critical theory, it was also a moment of jargonistic discourse. But it's important to do

what one can as an architect, critic, or spatial practitioner —
however we designate what we do — to speak to different
kinds of audiences. To think about it simply as "the public" is
wrong.

In my own criticism, I have three tiers: There's the tier of
October, where I can be as complicated as I want for an
audience of maybe three thousand. There's the tier of *Art
Forum* that has an audience of maybe twenty thousand, which
requires a different kind of language and one that I welcome.
And, then, in the *London Review of Books* I don't speak to
initiates, let alone experts, which takes a whole other kind of
language. But I think it's good for a writer to work in these
different ways. I like the different kinds of language that it
demands. But when Ben said, "there's no architecture without
a public," I thought, "Yes!" There's no writing without a public.
I always think about a reader. I have friends, critics, artists,
who say that's the last thing you should think about. But I
don't agree with Ben about originality. I don't see what I do as
avant-gardist at all. I'm much more interested in elucidation,
if not enlightenment. I think that's the key to resistance. This
is precisely why I got into architectural criticism. I was not
trained as an architect, but I studied architecture through
college and graduate school. People like me are dismissed
as uninformed. But architecture had become more and more
important, or important again, to public discourse and there
seemed to be such a gap between journalistic inanity and
insider criticism that it seemed important to engage questions
of architecture in another way.

Criticism, for me, is not about helping the architect advance.
It's mostly the opposite. But I do think criticism can help
change the terms of the architect-client conversation.
The New York Times went from Nicolai Ouroussoff to

Michael Kimmelman. Architects in this country and abroad are concerned that Kimmelman is not informed about architecture. He's a friend of mine, so I don't want to advocate. But he's smart and a very quick study and already, in his first few pieces of criticism, he's reset the terms of what counts as architectural and urban inquiry, at least for the *Times*. Ouroussoff really focused on the stars. I'm neither pro nor con; this is just what he did. Kimmelman hasn't discussed an architect that any of you would know, so far.

Whiting: Muschamp was also often criticized for favoring the stars, but I thought he was unusual in advancing both a social and a formal project within the newspaper world. I didn't always agree with him, but I thought he was one of the stronger critics we've had. The social and the formal aren't necessarily at odds.

Foster: I think that's right and I think Kimmelman will get there. I don't think the critic is secondary or belated, unlike most people. As a critic you're given what you're given and for Muschamp and even more for Ouroussoff that was what was given to them. In *The Art-Architecture Complex* I didn't necessarily want to begin with Rogers, Foster, and Piano, but they represent to me global styles of architecture that needed to be addressed in ways that I didn't think they were being addressed. But sometimes as a critic you just fall silent. If you're not in focus with respect to a given present you should fall silent. It happens to me all the time.

Whiting: There's an assumption that the architect can also fall silent, but it's actually very hard not to engage a client, especially when you're desperate to feed the mouths of your employees. That does appear to be a luxury of the critic. Obviously there are journalists who can't fall silent either, for the same reason. But the question of silence or the possibility of saying "no" isn't quite as easy as might be imagined in architecture.

JUDGMENT

Interview I

Ben van Berkel, Neil Denari, Hal Foster, Markus Miessen

Matthew Austin, Maria Batista, Kyle Byrne, Ana Victoria Chiari, Eunike, Clayton Fry, Ashley Hinton, Alexander Hohman, Kerim Miskavi, Maconda O'Connor, Chun Ou Yang, David Richmond, Jon Siani, Alex Tehranian, Louis Weiss, Sarah Whiting, Laura Williams

Alex Tehranian: Neil, it seems you often embrace architecture in two dimensions. With HL23, you flattened the structure onto the windows of the building. You embedded an aesthetic for the middle class into the windows and envelope of the Slavyanka City project. I have also heard you talk about reflected ceiling plans and the way people read them. Are you trying to spell out an argument for the public because it's easier to read the two-dimensional than the three-dimensional?

Neil Denari: My talk was, of course, edited to get at a point. In the High Line project I wouldn't want the story of the frit to be the tail that wagged the dog. It was an element that was reasonable to talk about at this event. The project itself, as a robust object sitting in a landscape, affecting urban space, operates in three dimensions probably far more viscerally than it does in two. Nevertheless, I do foreground the two-dimensional, from time to time, in order to talk about particular aspects of the work. Architecture tends toward one of two poles. It is either conceived as spectacle, bringing with it the problems of fetish and excess, or relegated to being a silent witness, a more or less inactive state. Between these poles there's obviously a big space to work in. We're trying to exploit that space. It's taboo to say we live in the two-dimensional. Actually, we always have, with forms of literature and communication and so forth. But it's more dramatic today. It's my small way of trying to say that I hope architecture won't be the medium of resistance or the guardian of the real, in the old sense. We're trying to incorporate conditions that may be psychologically related to the ephemeral world that everybody inhabits outside of space. If you counted the hours of the day that you inhabit that realm, it would be shocking. I'm trying to slip a different form of reality into architecture. I can't quite put my finger on how it works, or what its effects are, but I'm at least saying here's what the cultural purpose is. And I think it's important to foreground it. But the work is profoundly three-dimensional. Most people would call it sculptural. We don't draw it in two dimensions. I don't draw profiles and run off and build them. So, the answer to your question is yes and no.

Louis Weiss: I have an analogous question for Ben. I'm curious if you differentiate between after-images in the built work and the representation of the work in photographs and exhibitions. There's a difference between viewing a flat object and the experience of parallax walking through a building.

Ben van Berkel: It's difficult to describe how it works. The Mercedes-Benz Museum is perhaps the best example of how double-parallax images can be created. You can see the parallax as a moiré effect that generates one image after the other or an image produced by two images overlapping. In the Mercedes museum you have spaces that are behind one another, constantly creating layers of parallax effects. In the Harvard exhibition, I wanted to convey that three-dimensional spatial effect by projecting images across the two-dimensional walls of the space. I liked the idea that you stepped into the image. So, in the exhibition, it wasn't experimentation with surface alone. In some of our façades we work with double-layering so that, as you pass by the building, you think there is more plasticity. We are invested in the way the after-image creates double-readings. The after-images are not only pure images. They are reinterpretations. With the two dimensionality of the surface, we often refer to a notion discussed in the nineties: the idea of faciality. Faces have so many expressions and there are so many ways to look at a face. I've often thought faciality is a beautiful way to rethink what surfaces could do. How might you construct surfaces, even inside the building, in order to generate multiple effects and images?

Sarah Whiting: You overcome the problem of introducing the after-image into the exhibition, and you overcome it in terms of the facade, but what about in publications, which is where most of your work is understood?

Berkel: That's very difficult. It's always an attempt to assert the effects of the architecture through referential images. We have made several movies of our work. They are better at conveying the kaleidoscopic experience of the projects.

Tehranian: Ben, can we use the model of trained judgment for judging beauty?

Berkel: As you know, there is a long history of interpreting beauty. Often we have been unable to experience an aesthetic because it was new and unexpected or provocative such that we didn't understand it as aesthetic. Changing the boundaries between what is known as beautiful and what is not is very difficult. I'm flattered if someone says we make beautiful objects, but, in a sense, I'm also not. I'm more interested in what draws you into the project, instead of what is pleasing. Of course, I can give you examples where I discovered something that might become pleasing. For example, we used a form of serial geometric repetition in the Mobius House, purely for practical reasons, because we didn't want to have a builder who had to deal constantly with another casting technique. We used only four or five standard angles: seven degrees, nine degrees, eleven degrees, … But when you walk around the house, you discover an almost musical effect that offers incredible calmness despite its complexity. That was a discovery for me; an aesthetic principle for newness.

Ashley Hinton: Do two-dimensional drawings sufficiently represent those interesting spaces, or will we need new forms of representation in the future?

Berkel: We don't think through drawings anymore. We think in systems. You can rethink complexity by realizing that what you had in mind before is what complexity used to be. Complexity can also generate a new form of calmness. The reductive and complex can go together, support each other, and be part of the same system. When you reduce complex knowledge, you don't draw the plan of the building, you draw systems and information and you can do that today with so many means, not just the computer alone.

Denari: When you think about representation, one of the

most important things is the public. Typically, a project gets commissioned and then five renderings go out that ossifies the project until it's built. If it never gets built — eighty percent of what I do doesn't get built — then eighty percent of my production is ossified in certain types of images. You can curate that, but that's another conversation. In terms of process — and the issue of judgment — we're constantly making decisions about those renderings. We obviously have criteria that are guiding those decisions. In our office we do a lot of process renderings, rather than just looking at wireframes on a screen. There's a certain amount of information in a wireframe, but no affect. For somebody who's interested in controlling the project from a material point of view, it is unsatisfactory to know that even if we build it precisely we haven't controlled apprehension. You have to think about when the schedule makes decisions for you. Do you keep balls up in the air when you're looking at a plan or a diagram or data or a screenshot or a cardboard model and which ones? Everything has conditions and everything provides feedback.

Berkel: With today's knowledge, you have to invent ways of controlling the process. Neil draws systems too. In your presentation for the Slavyanka City project you had six types of windows; that's a system. In architecture today, one can play with seriality and variation more easily and intensely than ever before.

Markus Miessen: I think one needs to distinguish between the tools you're using and the audience you're presenting to. If you're doing a museum, you have to present to many different stakeholders and you need to think about the way you speak to these different audiences. It's not possible to produce one image or model that will make them all happy.

Denari: But I would argue that in the last seven or eight years — at least since the web reached its more saturated moment — the language of architectural drawing has become mainstream. The once private ways of communicating within the discipline are now increasingly understood by clients. Even within your own office, forms of communication are less proprietary than ever. It's interesting to consider whether or not we need to take back or reinvent some sort of architectural language to talk among ourselves, as opposed to having to use the images we talk to clients with. Our children are looking at images of three-dimensional models and diagrams on the web that they previously had no access to. Those representations will produce a literacy that is going to become important in the future.

Matthew Austin: Markus, I want to propose that there are formal components and effects in your work — the papers on the wall, the pamphlets, the arrangements of benches, a general do-it-yourself feel — that I associate with a "pop-up" propaganda or activism. It's an aesthetic that resonates with a younger generation and is a tactic deployed by other artists today.

Whiting: There is also an aesthetic to your written work and the research you presented yesterday. Even if there are differences among the built projects, there's a certain recognizability. It seems there is a generational code for radicality today.

Miessen: On my publications I always work with the same designer, Zak Kyes. We also collaborate on non-publication projects. He strongly believes in what he calls "economic design," which is partially a kind of rhetoric, because, quite often, you send him something and he asks you, "What do you want this to be?" You give him an idea or an instruction and the next day you basically get back what you asked him to do in a one to one translation. Some people would be disappointed and would ask, "What have you done?" I wouldn't have thought that there is a recognizable aesthetic, but, if there is, it's largely thanks to Zak and the fantastic team in my studio.

Hal Foster: Traditionally, the book is seen as a point of resolution and reflection, but you suggest it's a moment in a process. Do you have any qualms about this de-resolution of the book form? If it's not generational, it comes down to the milieu: you, Hans Ulrich Obrist, and a few others. If it's not about participation, it's about collaboration.

Miessen: My books are not a final statement or written version of a belief system that's set and is not going to change. They are steps in a process. I basically throw something on the table; that starts a conversation and leads to something else. I'm launching a new book, *Waking Up From the Nightmare of Participation*. I asked a group of people to critically reflect on *The Nightmare of Participation* and promised them that whatever they would write, no matter how critical of my work, it wouldn't be edited. There is already an epilogue to *The Nightmare of Participation*, in which I asked Carson Chan to review the book within the book itself. It's a way of furthering a conversation.

Whiting: Hal, can you distinguish how *The Art-Architecture Complex* differs?

Foster: In all possible ways! Markus, I thought it was extraordinary to have within the book a critique of the project. It didn't seem to me preemptive or prophylactic. I really admired it.

Eunike: Markus, you describe the nightmare of collaboration when there is no censor and no editing. Isn't that what you're promoting?

Miessen: Of course there is some kind of editorial process. There is certainly editing at the moment you set up a project and choose certain people to write about something. But, with respect to what you called censorship: promising that the text would not be edited in terms of content was, in this particular case, very important. The generation of today craves that things won't be edited out.

Maconda O'Connor: Hal, do you think the commodification of architecture is mutually exclusive with criticality?

Foster: Here's my two-minute rap on commodification. I have more experience with art schools than architecture schools, but artists tend to start out as expressionists, then they discover the market and become cynics, because they think commodification is total. "Commodification" is a word, like "spectacle," that means too much and too little. Art has been a commodity since easel painting and maybe even before. Since David, artists have circulated in the marketplace more than through commissions. And by the time of Courbet, that's the way it is. Once the old structure of patronage — the clergy, the aristocracy — breaks down, it's the marketplace. So I try not to use the term "commodification" because it over-determines. I think architecture is a different matter. It has clients who establish constraints: conditions, program, etc. But these constraints also free architecture from outright commodity status. It's the same thing for a critic. Criticism emerges with the public sphere, but this isn't really an historical moment;

it's an ideal or heuristic idea that there should be a sphere where anything could be discussed. A well-known version of this space is/was the newspaper, which has always been framed by commercial enterprise. The commodity is just another delivery system. This is not to celebrate it; but it concerns me when young people confront this idea and are so overwhelmed by it that they think "I can't do anything" or "I'll just make the coolest product I can." Everyone, including the critic, has to navigate the marketplace. Critical theory itself has long been part of market structures.

O'Connor: Is our culture of instant gratification bringing that commodification to a new level?

Foster: We're in this moment, technically and commercially, where information can be designed and redesigned, and sold and resold, continually. So, in a way, even though this is an ongoing process, you have to articulate each new installation of your thought. This is, in part, why I hold onto the old form of the book, which is perfectly a commodity too. I'm into slow products, because we're asked to buy the same black t-shirt every three weeks or so.

Denari: We began the conversation talking about beauty. But I have to ask myself as an architect: What's the interest level in what I do? What am I trying to put out to the public and does it devolve into entertainment? As a member of the public, looking at an architect's work, I might conclude one work reaches a fever pitch of interest, or another is over-saturated and I lose interest, or nothing is going on and I don't have any interest. In what I do I'm obviously making aesthetic judgments about the work, more than engaging the question of interest *a priori*. I have to let that go and then put the work into the public realm. It's always distressing when spectacle becomes the benchmark for judgment. That fault line is too little or too much. I think that's a big issue, especially politically, relative to how we think about our work. If there's a strong conversation today about the question of how architects approach work, by whatever direction we get there, it dares to take the question of interest into consideration as opposed to the other possibility that claims — through data, or some other method — an automatic kind of design.

Weiss: I wonder whether, relative to architecture, the quest for legibility sits at the intersection of value and interest. Hal was talking about either having or not having a reader in mind when you're writing. If interest is at issue, you have the legibility of what you're designing in mind relative to the subject.

Laura Williams: Do you think HL23 was successful because you have a captive audience on the High Line, or do you think the two-dimensional structural frit could operate legibly within another context?

Denari: That was a particular move that you need to keep in the context of other projects. I'm not trying to diagram or explain something so didactically. It was a moment where we could use an interesting historical notion of structural expression — I wouldn't say expressionism — because it related to what the building was doing. "If legibility is the answer, what's the question?" If we're in a world where there's no storytelling, it's trying to be Frank Stella's "What you see is what you see." At other times, one wants legibility to have a relationship to media and reading and that doesn't only come through propositions of the two-dimensional or a building that is read as a logo or cartoon. In other words, one wants the work to be easily digestible as media. Legibility is a default for writers, graphic designers, and others. It represents, at one level, communication. For those who might want to say they're not interested in legibility, then architecture is a post-communication project in which you make the audience work hard. Honestly, I don't know where I stand, if the question of legibility is the answer. Given the answer, I'm not sure I know what the question is. But I'm deeply interested in the conversation and in working that way in architecture. On a personal level, I think empathy generates attraction and is about connectivity and I'm putting empathy into the realm of legibility to invoke and problematize media and architecture's role as media. I do that intentionally, as opposed to just saying I'm interested in the sublime, the beautiful, the sculptural, or the precise.

Williams: Hal, I'm interested in your thoughts on legibility. You talked about how you cater to different audiences in your writings. Do you think that if I were to pick up an article that wasn't quite meant for me that I ought to be able to comprehend it?

Foster: I think the question concerns the public dimensions — the public address — of architecture, or criticism, or anything. I think that's absolutely crucial. I support Neil's idea that there should be a distinction between legibility and image-ability. That said, there's plenty of room for legibility between structural expression or structural transparency and image-ability. There are all kinds of ways to be legible. I'm personally committed to an idea of structural transparency, but that's the old modernist in me. It was very important to the art and architecture that first engaged me. There used to be a rough equation in the modernist project between the different kinds of transparency in art and architecture, which was essentially: "I will show you materials, I will show you my structures, I will show you my process, and my production. That will allow you to reflect on your own materials, structures, processes, and production." That engagement is against the obfuscation of other kinds of image-ability. In other words, it's part of a public sphere. It suggests that if architecture can be transparent, politics and social relations might be too. That's a very strong idea in modernisms that insist on transparency.

The problem now is that transparency has become its own obfuscation. For Norman Foster to put a dome on the Reichstag, with the intention that you can look down and see the legislators at work, is a bit of a joke. But I think legibility is absolutely crucial. The irony, in terms of art, is that the move to render production transparent made the work more hermetic. There are numerous moments when construction is exposed, for example, in Russian constructivism. But that exposure befuddled people in the work of minimalists and post-minimalists. The minimalist project was, in a way, a constructivist recovery: an effort to make everything transparent. Richard Serra still attempts this. But that project was often pursued through deskilling: it is not only transparent, but easy — I'll show you what I do, in the doing. Deskilling was a way to open the work of art, but it often made the work more hermetic than not. So, it's a tricky question, but I think it's an essential one. I'd much rather be lucid than interesting. For me, writing is a question of how to elucidate.

Denari: It's a good point about transparency turning to abstraction. The ambition to disclose produced an alienating moment especially with early modernism. Modernists disclosed a wall, or where the windows were, or where the door was, and it messed people up, because they weren't in the place you thought they'd be. That is one of the tremendous ironies bound to operate in any project that tries to be clear or come clean. And this may be part of the curiosity of this symposium: Is it possible to convert the potential for alienation into forms of attraction, lucidity, or interest that are powerful, rather than gratuitous or excessive? That's the fault line we're on today. Everybody's trying to find or legitimate arguments for that, because that's what the culture is calling for as architecture is drawn into or returning to that political dimension. We're all trying to figure out how to do it cogently rather than belligerently and avoid obfuscation and the hermetic. Those historical legacies are there and we're trying to battle them in a way. There's an attempt to create systems of legibility, but it's a question of both storytelling and content. What I do is very different than British high-tech. Even though one might loosely throw me in that category from time to time, it's definitely a different cultural agenda. In Norman Foster's Hearst Tower, he signals the structural frame, but the frame of the building is within the skin. In HL23 our structure is behind and could have been left completely unconnected to the glass. I'm sure Norman Foster wouldn't have done what I did, because it goes into the realm of decoration. Our approach was an interpretation of modernist discourse that he wouldn't advocate.

Foster: If you're an architect, an artist, or a writer today, you have to project a public; you can't presume one. One of the extraordinary things about the bourgeois culture that produced these different modernisms is that it had a patron class — an enfranchised bourgeoisie that wanted to be challenged and took the idea of critique seriously. The history of art is full of engaged patrons who wanted to have that alienation effect, if not to be alienated. In the last couple of decades, it seems to me, there is a change in the very social structure of support for art, architecture, and writing. That's a problem that is perhaps beyond us all. Future practitioners will need to engage their peers in the importance of their projects as they develop. One of the reasons I'm at Princeton is that it interests me to be a professor of the next American ruling class. I'm in the business of the production of the patrons of things as much as the production of practitioners.

Berkel: I like this discussion of the phenomenon of alienation. We don't have to apologize as architects. I hope that what I said about science yesterday is not misunderstood. If you take, for instance, a painter like Seurat, he was an incredible alienator. He represented the world in a way that even photography had not presented yet. But he learned from photography and was interested in the science of optics. He misinterpreted the science and, in a sense, invented with mistakes. That's what I support. You are in the fields of science and art when you are an architect and you can learn from your peers. But you can also misinterpret it, to alienate, and we shouldn't apologize for that.

Kerim Miskavi: Do you think the public should understand the framework in which the building was designed in order to critique it, or should critique only occur after experiencing the building?

Denari: That's a question that's often asked but it reverts to the idea of what the building communicates. Peter Eisenman tried to discipline process into the project and make a language out of it. If you take my experience of Mercedes Benz: I knew the project. I studied it before I went. I read every book and went as a member of the public to see the project. Of course, I was completely informed, but I wasn't carrying the plans around. I wasn't a prospector with a treasure map, trying to find the good and the bad things. But, obviously, a project based on circulation is a diagram of itself and will therefore telegraph itself without the architects having to explain it.

Berkel: The Benz Museum is not a built diagram. There are often discussions concerning what the diagram can do relative to built form, but the most important thing is to know how to instrumentalize the diagram; how to translate it; how to rethink the way you notate as generating prolific possibilities for the way you design architecture. In the contemporary re-conception of the diagram, it's not reductive. It's not the modernist principle of the diagram.

Tehranian: A number of architects, instead of turning a diagram into a building, turn the building into a diagram. It's almost generating the absurd. Is there an aspect of this absurdity that creates alienation?

Berkel: Yes, it's around. It's a building that becomes a cartoon. It's not the architecture we're going to stand for. It's a form of provocation, but it gives you, in my opinion, a very short effect. It's a one-liner. And it's bad for architecture, because one-liners are only good if the building exists only for a day.

Foster: But aren't you interested in where the building expresses the technique — to put it as reductively as possible — as opposed to the function? I'm very interested in architecture that diagrams its own techniques, its own processes. There's a lot of space between that reduction, or schematization, and the absurdist cartoon that can be developed from it.

Berkel: I never said that. Techniques are there to rediscover and reinvent what you then translate or transport into a spatial or organizational principle. I'm not arguing that tools, or the way you work with tools, should be expressed in architecture. I'm interested in the way architecture can generate a plurality of unfolding readings, beyond the phenomenon of collage. We know collage is a modern project — allowing one to distinguish the origin of parts. I hope you cannot find that in my work. You can't see what is structure or understand the spatial organization in relationship to what you gain when you move through and experience the project. That's why I talk about parallax views and ways of reading. Proliferation is more important than reduction.

Denari: I don't want to say all diagrammatic architecture is secretly interested in forms, whether it's immediately consumed, or otherwise. But, to engage Hal's question, it begs of the author a certain calculation. And that's good. Everybody always has a project about form. Yet the extent to which anybody's going to risk talking about form, in the way Ben is talking about parallax, has nothing to do with the diagram and everything to do with a whole variety of processes about designing. I don't think architecture that operates from a diagram is necessarily under-representing the complexity of design. But when it does, the architect has probably worked very hard to conceal the complexities that go into that architecture. Frank Gehry will tell you, when he makes one volume sit on top of another volume, how hard it is to detail it so that it looks like that. It's why people say it's so hard to build minimal work, because everything has to be concealed and hidden. Diagrammatic work is a forced arrangement that is cultural and political. As architects we're always interested in who's willing to say what about those kinds of processes and it ultimately does have something to do with the public and what they know and understand about the work. It goes back to this idea of whether it's didactic.

Do you need a manual to understand these projects and agendas?

Foster: To call it didactic is to suggest it's somehow authoritative, that it's about authorship, whereas the impulse behind a relation, if not an expression, of technique is to de-mythologize the author, the artist, or the architect. That's consistent in the move towards transparency in twentieth century art, which comes at a moment when artists want to get away from the idea of genius. That's really important in the question of public address. It's not read in terms of Gehry, the great image-maker.

How Hard Can It Be?

Jeffrey Kipnis

Influence

The informal way architects communicate with one another requires that we do not legally or formally acknowledge our influences because it stops the course of influences. My job, as a critic, is to judge that. That's the most interesting and the only legitimate form of judgment at the level of the discipline.

Bad

There are two prevailing models of judgment that I think are really bad. The first model is building type analysis. It is the single biggest problem in architecture. The second standard bad idea is the scholarly art-historical approach, which studies the work of one artist or architect; although if you learn to compare one work to another that approach can be more interesting.

Masterpiece

When I say, "Is OMA's Seattle Library a good library?" you say "How hard can it be to make a big thing that you can walk into, find some books, and walk out?" If Seattle is a great library, then the Marcel Breuer library in Atlanta is a horrible library because it does exactly the opposite work. I want to know: What it is about our discipline that considers both of those to be masterpieces?

Type

Architects don't design prisons anymore — you can't leave the security of the neighbors open to the unpredictable imaginations of an architect. We don't design hospitals anymore. Soon we're not going to design schools. Losing schools will be a big problem. Boutique specializations come in with a team of experts: a psychologist, a safety expert, a legal expert, a cost evaluator, ...; a team that does nothing but schools. And they will win every argument about reproducing the banal mediocrity of a pretty good school because that's actually what nearly everybody wants. The idea that there's some advantage to an architectural project for a school that's made of something like dropped cubes is very difficult to argue when boutique specializations are using BIM to make real-time decisions about cost-effectiveness. So, the single worst way to judge a building, from the point of view of architecture, is building type specialization. Yet everyone does it — every teacher, every student, and even I do it. It's hard not to.

Scholarship

If you're an expert on one practice, that's an okay way to judge, but it's probably not as important today as it might have been at one time. It over-valorizes the intentions and craft of a single architect and does us no good. It particularly does the critic no good. For about twenty years, critics have done nothing but read what the architect has to say about their buildings and repeat it in better language.

Longevity

A better way — also standard, but a better way — to understand buildings is to engage long-lived problems in architecture that have produced creative histories. For example: the question of how a building meets the ground or the sky, or the corner problem. That's a better approach, because it lets you avoid paying attention to the work of a single architect or building type.

For example, instead of considering concert halls as a type, you could consider how they meet the ground. The Musikverein in Vienna meets the ground solidly, with a neoclassical attitude about land. Frank Gehry's Disney Concert Hall has a similar pyramid form and materiality, but it is comparatively larger at the bottom and smaller at the top; so, in a relaxed way, it's reinforcing the ground. OMA's Casa da Música states its decision to not be a part of the ground and therefore not be a part of Porto.

Dialectic

I don't actually believe architecture has ever had the dialectic structure: Modern vs. Post-Modern. There were hegemonic institutional practices that politically controlled the discourse to our advantage, like the Greys and the Whites. Yet the whole time the Greys and the Whites were arguing on the East coast, the California School was developing a completely new idea of the part-to-whole relationship without any discourse, without any Institute for Architecture and Urban Studies, and it produced what I think is the most influential architecture to come out of the United States: Thom Mayne, Frank Gehry, and Eric Moss.

Commonplace

Not only is art changing our relationship to the commonplace, the commonplace changes our relationship to art. That makes it absolutely impossible to discipline communication and influence using any notion of judgment.

Change

In architecture and the arts — discourses that, unlike the sciences or law, are not grounded in strong decision-making — you want to encourage deviation. There's going to be a conversation between the past and the present, but the past is not going to authorize or authenticate the present. It will not produce continuity. You have to have change to produce continuity.

I Can't See a Thing

Sylvia Lavin

Everywhere

There is a lot of criticism producing judgment all around us today: every blog, every newspaper, … It's as though "everyone's a critic," but now, really, everyone is a critic. It's a do-it-yourself criticism. There are mass quantities of criticism and therefore constant judgment. Yet, none of it has much importance. It's ubiquitous and yet invisible at the same time.

Travel

Quatremère de Quincy was criticized for being an armchair archaeologist because he would write entire books on Egyptian architecture without ever coming within two thousand miles of the Nile. But he also contributed significantly to the idea that travel would be a way to become a proper critic. It was only through travel — in this case, to Rome — where you could breathe in the sky, the earth, the climate, the natural forms and the style of the buildings, the games, the festivals, the clothing, … all those atmospheres that could turn the tasteless amateur into a critic. Travel was a means of obtaining primary experience; experience that turns the critic into a judge.

We know that Ruskin was the first architect to travel with a (massive) camera. You can't imagine the mediation that must have taken place between him and that gondolier; you put that camera on that gondola and he would have been at the bottom of the Grand Canal.

Site

The question of judgment comes down — in a metaphorical way — to the question of the site visit. Privileging the site visit is one of the few things common to almost every position operating today. The site visit resonates deeply with lingering phenomenologists, who surround us with their attachment to smells and the poetry of experience. I would say the site visit is very important to critical theorists, who, despite themselves, often maintain an innocent sense of the primacy of an encounter with the object. And I would also say the site visit is currently re-emerging as an issue for what we might call post-critical critics who want the object to trigger new feelings. So I think the site visit is, in fact, at the heart of the crisis of judgment.

Blindness

So how do we think about field trips today? Here is Bob Venturi, recently, in Rome. He appears to be looking at ... nothing at all! He's tired and sleepy, with his eyes closed. Somehow we're moving around a lot but have become, in a certain way, blind. There is an important tradition of the blind critic. It perhaps begins with Denis Diderot, who wrote a letter on blind judgment. He believed he could demonstrate that everyone, including blind people, saw in perspective and that perspective was, in fact, not a natural perceptual condition. He was trying to assert that vision was a cultural construct.

There is still, to this day, a kind of blind critic, and I think that's a big problem for criticism as a whole, wherein emphasis on "the techniques of the observer" — if we use Jonathan Crary's term — makes everybody blind because the object doesn't matter.

Endless

There's another view of blindness, which is not that it doesn't matter what you see, because everyone sees the same thing, but that in seeing we proliferate endless numbers of things. There is the famous Indian proverb of the seven blind men, who all go up and touch the elephant and, of course — quite to the contrary of Diderot — produce different descriptions.

The apparent choice is either no elephant or the same elephant, and a whole range of elephants in between.

Any criticism that can't engage that variation, it seems to me, has a problem.

Bump

Some years ago I wrote a piece about Preston Scott Cohen's proposed Tel Aviv Museum of Art. The building recently opened and I was invited to go see it. I had a number of commitments to write and talk about the building and I knew the kinds of things these audiences wanted to know — for example, how a straight glass railing will meet a curved wall; the adhesive between the two is not strong enough to adhere the glass to the curving concrete. The architect would never show photos of this, nor of the devices that prevent people from banging their head on the inclined surfaces.

Having traveled there, I couldn't help but bump into these conflicts. My being there produced not judgments but a proliferation of different objects and perceptions that I couldn't align.

Oops

If we think about the very long project — the corner problem, for example — I would like to think that a hundred years from now nobody would think Brunelleschi fucked up the Pazzi Chapel because a little piece of the pilaster is left over. At present, this is a profound reflection on the difference between architecture as a project and architecture as a building process. If we think about this again, we can be moved by the one to reconsider the other.

Constraint

Judgment should be constrained, rendered momentarily absolute, rather than relative, by the particularities of the object.

Distance

How far am I willing to go? Right now I'm willing to go to Australia to see an installation by Thomas Demand.

The job of judgment should be to support the object in its effort to proliferate — to be constituted as a multitude of objects — and to share the burden of the consequences of that proliferation, which might well be to weaken the object's autonomy. The effect of judgment is to interrupt the current state of the diffuse global citizen, which, it seems to me, has supplanted the once-argued position of critique. I now think of the field trip as a source of this proliferation of the object and hence of the validities of judgment. Thomas Demand's work — the photos, the models of photos of things that he's taken while travelling, producing the thing, making the photo — is a way of provoking new experiences rather than confirming old ones. It's important to think of the site visit not as a means to mythologize the single phenomenal experience but, rather, as one experience producing an apparatus among many.

Naked

Many of you know that in 1969, as Adorno was about to begin a lecture, just as he was clearing his throat, a group of female students came into the room and exposed their breasts to him. He was very poorly equipped to deal with this and was utterly silenced. This man, who produces the notion of criticism, and without whom these girls probably would have had no idea what critique and resistance might have meant, was reduced to a kind of silence, if you will, by the force of the naked.

Me

I'll conclude with an aborted field trip to Demand's studio.
I found it extremely off-putting that he had papered the
windows of his studio to block the view. He doesn't want
anybody to see all those models inside. So, in this case, I was
stopped; I was blinded. At that moment I felt a kind of reversal,
which is to say that, rather than judge, I felt an interest in
thinking about those things judging me. The kind of judgment I
produce might in turn be reflected back on my own state. And
that's exactly the kind of thing I'm interested in.

Speech

On the one hand, judgment is the easiest thing to do, but maybe it's the hardest thing to talk about. I want to lay out the issue of how to judge and how we decide between the poles of "doing" and "saying" — in particular, through the idea of the speech act: a specific kind of saying that is also a doing. I'll undertake this with regard to the formation of community and audiences, both as a critic and as a director, which is now my practice. My design practice is the design of a school.

Act

Jeff and Sylvia's presentations this morning were laid out in terms of architecture's score and its performance. I'm interested in how — through the idea of the speech act — we could think of the problem of score and performance through writing and criticism. Is there a difference between score and performance in writing as there is in architecture? Are writing and criticism different kinds of practices that don't operate around those two terms? That is to say, is there, through the speech act, a way to think about the relationship between score and performance in architecture in a different way than we do when we traditionally think about the relationship of drawing to building?

Do

As critics, teachers, administrators, and designers — as your former governor would say — "We're the deciders." That's what we do. So my first inclination is to invoke Barnett Newman, who, when he was asked about aesthetics, said, "What do the birds care of ornithology?" What do the deciders care about judgment? We just do it. We decide. We perform it.

Market

I'll cite William Burroughs: "As one judge said to another, 'Be just and if you can't be just, be arbitrary.'" That's my motto for judgment and I've been consistently true to the second part at least. The gloss to this advice: How do critics deploy a random act? By random, I don't mean chance. Obviously, this is the kind of random that you have to be very precise and intentional about. In a certain sense, that allows critics to find new values and new forms of knowledge. In other words: How do we make opportunities from market inefficiencies, specifically in the market of criticism — the critical market — and the academic market?

Taste

I would introduce two more unfashionable words into that decision-making: taste and intuition.

If you raise the problem of taste, you have to invoke Charlie the Tuna, the problem of good taste versus tasting good: evaluation versus performance, knowing versus being. It's a split between saying "I have good taste" and simply tasting good. Inevitably, StarKist would send a message down to Charlie the Tuna — "Sorry, Charlie." Maybe this is the state of criticism: if you don't taste good, you can at least have good taste and live to tell about it. Maybe all critics are condemned to being told "Sorry, Charlie," and convincing people who taste good to say "Charlie sent you."

Know

*I was invited to give a talk at the administrator's conference
of the ACSA. The theme was "Old School — New School." We
were asked to give a brief summation of what architects need
to know. That seemed fine. I said "Yes." I love doing manifestos.
I don't really care so much about what architects need to
know — that sounded like the metric of evaluative bureaucracy:
provide a check list of what an architect needs to know — but I
figured I could avoid that part ...*

Laundry

... then we were asked to present how architecture schools should respond to the challenges posed by changes such as globalization, the environment, emergent technology, social and economic equity, to mention a few from outside the field.

I was struck by this laundry list. It represents the thematization of architecture education and that's precisely the problem. I was invited to represent the "New School," but, if this was what the "New School" was about, I was clearly "Old School."

As with the original, pre-themed, Legos, The Old School for me is one where you can change the world, or, more precisely, make any world, with three colors and one shape. That's all you need.

Dunno

We need to take seriously that the highest compliment paid to an architect, critic, or theorist is: "You don't know what you're talking about." In academia we hear that phrase all the time. In practice you hear it. You certainly hear it as a critic. If you're a theorist you hear it a lot. We never know what we're talking about. And we should say, "You know, you're right; and that's a badge of honor." We actually don't know what we're talking about and that's the beauty of a projective practice. It doesn't exist until we say it. It's not about matching the world of facts; it's about imagining a new world that we can inhabit as designers and architects and critics. It's our job description to not know what we're talking about. Talking about it makes it so.

New

Do we want to imagine new worlds or reconfirm existing worlds?

Admire

The image of the four earths is supposed to make us feel bad. If everybody consumed like we do, we'd need more than four earths to survive.

But, as a designer and a politically incorrect politician, you need to read that image against the grain.

That's really cool: four Earths!

It's making you feel bad, but you also have to admire it as an act of design: "You're right. We need more Earths, damn it!"

Value

How do you bet on something that doesn't yet have a market?

How do you look at the field, divide it up, and realize that something is being undervalued?

That's what you do as a critic. You figure out where the low value is and you put your chips on it.

Judgment Day

Brett Steele

Definition

A young Swiss architect confronts a new form of construction. He converts that construction into a diagram that became foundational for an entire century's definition of modern architectural judgment. Today, this is how we judge the difference between that particular architectural mind and the many other lesser minds proposing similar-looking concrete structures around 1915. Le Corbusier's talent was forged by the rarest kind of judgment: that needed to change other architectural minds.

Unbelievable

I'm interested in the utility architects derive from entirely false lives; from inadequate, unbelievable examples of architectural judgment. Far more than forming a career (which for many is challenge enough), genuine talent triangulates and directs an entire discipline through forms of judgment that are entirely fictitious and useful to no one but themselves, though the success of those judgments is often measured by how others use them ... or don't.

Conspiracy

Critics, like most cultural producers, are much less important in the communication of ideas than they've been at other times in the history of our discipline. Agency today lies in the audience — this is the culprit truly responsible for the post-(post-)modern "death of the author." And this is why conspiracy theory remains the only viable form of theory today. Conspiracies allow knowledge to travel not just in new and unexpected ways, but also to be manufactured, bent, and erased in unreal — even unimaginable — ways.

Confession

In my many years as a project architect, a project planner, a manager, a teacher, a studio critic, and now school director, I have never before thought about the topic of judgment. For me, you just do it. It's like breathing. So let me make a first, honest confession: convening an architectural symposium to discuss "judgment" feels like being a fish and trying to talk about water. Let's just swim.

Interpret

A building might be thought of in one way by its architect, in another way by the engineer, in a third way by an occupant, client, or even passerby. That is to say, there are accounts that lie parallel to and sometimes at odds with the architect's own judgment of a building. This might be one way of grasping why judgment seems such a poor means by which to convey the idea of architectural knowledge, which has long been the province of an incredibly small number of believers.

Archive

The evolution of architecture schools — from the great courtyard of the École des Beaux-Arts to today's elastic, electronic archives — reveals a transformation in the communicative imperatives of architectural knowledge and its discipline. What was once stored in the dead rocks of the classical carvings displayed in the École flicker today in the digital files transmitted across networks at the speed of light.

The difference is one of degree, not kind.

Trauma

There's more to gain by observing bad judgment than good.

Architects don't often talk about their mistakes. They tend to avoid them at all costs. Kengo Kuma's M2 building, constructed at the height of the Tokyo real estate bubble in the early nineties, was so horribly bad that it almost single-handedly led to the death of Post-Modernism. Kuma was so traumatized by this building that he spent two years writing about Bruno Taut and his experiences to that point in his career, leading to his essay "The Anti-Object," a rare example of an architect critically assessing his own mid-career failure. That publication allowed Kuma to re-invent himself into the figure many of you know today, a figure more introspective, judgmental, and worldly in both personal and disciplinary ways.

Transfer

Schools are much more machines for transmitting and broadcasting judgment than delivering or manufacturing knowledge. In many ways, making audiences is a more important project for an architecture school than making architects.

Rational

I dismiss the idea that judgment is related in any way to rational thinking or definitive knowledge. Facts today are too easy to design and fabricate. Performance — how things move — matters more than form. Le Corbusier's Modulor Man has long been supplanted by today's architect in motion.

Conversation II

Jeff Kipnis, Sylvia Lavin, Bob Somol, Brett Steele, Sarah Whiting

Lars Lerup, Albert Pope, Bryony Roberts, Joseph Scherer, among others.

Sarah Whiting: Let's begin by considering how seeing a building *in situ* as opposed to seeing a representation of a building affects judgment. The field trip has the downfalls you pointed out, Sylvia, such as mythologizing, and, Jeff, you have also questioned the need to experience a building in person. But seeing a building in the flesh is undeniably immediate, even visceral. Should this make a difference?

Sylvia Lavin: When critics attend to the multiple ontologies of the object qua object and collapse them into a diagram of a disciplinary problem, we become vulnerable to fetishistic attachments to the primacy of experience. That leads to Michael Kimmelman saying, "I wish there was more room for my bicycle in Manhattan," and calling that architectural criticism. The attachment to experience is the companion evil to the professional positivism Jeff was talking about.

They both undermine the disciplinary conceptual project. The issue of experience is one that interests me in particular, although I think it parallels professional practice in another way. Experience or affect — that whole vocabulary — is now something that is used by what you might call the Right and the Left within architecture.

Jeffrey Kipnis: A hysterical exaggeration of the importance of effects is crucial if there is to be a disciplinary argument. Only the exaggeration of the significance of minor effects lends value to any judgment. That's why Sylvia is absolutely correct in discussing the site. I don't expect anyone to come away with anything on a site visit unless they're involved in the architectural problem.

My argument about specific attention to small problems is genre based. The materialist analysis of architecture has, over the last thirty years, blossomed into an entire ecology of genres. Theory hasn't been able to cope. Whether it should or shouldn't is an interesting question. There is a spectrum of judgments. If you believe the field of judgment is a question of guilt or innocence, right or wrong, you cannot possibly engage any form of art today. Nor can you be naïve about its production. For example, in some works of architecture, in order to get the architectural effect, you have to not be there. It's important to know things that you cannot get in the presence of the work because the architectural project is directed against presence. Peter Eisenman's Monument to the Murdered Jews, for example. So I think Sylvia was correct in saying we have collapsed two important, but different, ideas: one is affect and the other is experience. Experience means you're an adequate recipient and judge of your own pleasures, which is probably true. But it doesn't make you a judge of architecture. In order for there to be affect, it has to be culturally grounded in a specific set of circumstances over and beyond experience. Like a good soundtrack, most of architecture has its most interesting effects precisely when you're not paying attention to it; if I call your attention to it, it's ruined.

Whiting: I think the spectrum of effects is an interesting point. But I'd be careful not to discard dealing with the building as an object. Our recent architectural understanding has been dominated by modes of representation and its reading as opposed to architectural problems coming through the project.

Lavin: The architectural project is largely articulated through modes of representation. I wouldn't want to validate representation over the object. But I would want to treat that system of representation as an object. That requires attention to the limits of representation. But we don't want to make vulnerable the very discipline that we want to support by not allowing those different modalities — the object, the representational, the constructive, the professional, the material etc. — to each develop their own robust internal system of eminence.

In terms of the built thing, there's no need to collapse the observer and the object. There is a branch of criticism produced by the architect that I would consider internal to the ontology of the object. In that case, there's often not enough distance from the object. The sociality of judgment comes when it's one against another. So the object is proliferated and has many modalities of representation, of which the criticism produced by the architect is one. Internal design decisions are not what I would consider judgment in the sense that we're talking about it today. I say that as a provocation because often there is no object: we either displace the object into the problem of representation or we're internal to the logic of the object.

Kipnis: If I was a music critic I'd be looking at the score, but every once in a while I'd like to hear a performance. I think of buildings as the single performance of a particular score. Seeing Scott Cohen's building ruined it for me. I was appalled — not that I don't think Scott's building is a great building; it's not only a great project, it's a great building. But so much was disturbing. I came away sorry I'd made the visit. I would prefer to just study scores, but, given a chance to see performances, it's always something I should do. I don't know that I've ever been convinced that anybody has ever gotten anything out of visiting a building that they didn't already get out of it before they went.

Lavin: I think you're diminishing the cultural power associated with a visit to the object.

Joseph Scherer: Sylvia, do you think your sense that the audience anticipates a particular critique — a particular judgment — of Scott Cohen's building is linked to a cultural claim about the state of judgment today? I'm wondering to what degree we want the public to be talking about the corner you discussed?

Lavin: I would say a good critic anticipates their audience. You can be really dull in one context and interesting in another depending on your audience. I do think judgments need to be understood within a field of discourse and that's important in the sense that they're not absolute. But I think the question invokes a false distinction between "the public" and the "architectural audience." Most of the architectural audience would see the glass railing in Scott's building as a mistake. If the architectural audience is going to see that as a mistake, what am I expecting from "the public"? They're the same.

Kipnis: By the time you think something is important enough to do, it's ridiculous. With respect to the glass issue Sylvia discussed: so it's a mistake. But if you're really worried about it — if you're really thinking about it — then you see the positive possibilities. Sylvia asked an important question: What is the good of negative judgment in architecture? You can understand a journalistic negative criticism, because after you read it you don't go to see a movie or buy a book. But the worst thing you can say about a building is nothing; just be indifferent, which is what we are to most buildings all the time. I would rather set something into motion by paying close, ridiculous attention to the small details of a building and jump to conclusions in a positive sense, rather than exercising negative judgments, because I cannot understand what value it would have.

Bryony Roberts: Sylvia, today you're talking about the distance between the viewer and the object and the layering of critical and disciplinary awareness in experience. But in *Kissing Architecture* you prioritize the physical experience of the artwork — it's the body of the viewer but also the body of the artist, Pipiloti Rist, that's disrupting the space. I'm wondering if you see the body as an important element in disrupting architectural practices?

Lavin: What I'm saying today doesn't exclude the analysis of experience as a produced event. In *Kissing Architecture* I tried not to suggest that I was affirmed in some embodied way — which is the embodied perception problem of minimalism — but rather that my sense of what I could be was transformed.

It's not affirming; a new thing is produced in that moment.

Kipnis: It's not the idea that you're stable and you're now having new perceptions. That's Kantian. It's the idea that you're transformed. You're no longer the thing that came into the space. That's a crucial distinction.

Lavin: Yes, it's a crucial distinction. That is partly what I meant when I said it's interesting to think of buildings judging us. If we're so interested in the effects of architecture, one instrument I have to measure that effectiveness is my own reconstitution *at that moment*. But I'm entitled to have a different Self at a different moment and to change my mind, up to a point, or to say that my reconstituted Self is now free to witness other things that it wouldn't have witnessed before.

There was a lot of interesting discussion today about judgment and fiction — producing space between the notion of judgment and truth would be another way to put it. But we should also talk about the difference between cognition and judgment, because there were lots of issues there. Brett, in particular, was thinking about modes of thought and modes of making decisions, which is not quite the same thing as modes of producing value. I was on the lookout — and I hope somebody was looking at me, because I'm sure I did it — for terms of value that were left without judgment. There were certain terms — beauty, ugly, aesthetic, good and bad — that were used in passing and were, perhaps unconsciously, left without discussion.

Kipnis: In his analysis of the Glass House and the Farnsworth House, Kenneth Frampton was dedicated to making one good and one evil. One is tectonic and the other was scenographic. He wanted the scenographic to be immoral and the tectonic to have a moral dimension. What's incredible about that article is that he succeeded in convincing me that both of those things were true: one was tectonic and the other was scenographic. But he didn't succeed in convincing me that one was good and one was bad. For me, that ended the possibility of judgments on moral or ethical terms and set into motion the possibility that architecture could begin to produce new kinds of genres. If you're interested in an egalitarian project, or at least a project that speaks to a larger number of people more intimately, you have to experiment with a proliferation of genres. It's far more interesting than good versus bad and all the things you said we may have metaphysically used as judgments. I don't see what good and bad can do in the field. Our job as teachers is really simple. To recognize the problem is the beginning of expertise. We teach works of genius. We break them down into simple pedagogical exercises so that we can teach them as exercises in mediocrity. We produce an increasingly mediocre world of expertise, so that new expertise and genius can emerge.

Brett Steele: The claim that architecture is increasingly trying to talk to a larger audience requires defending when it feels as though we're also at a moment in which architecture culture, like so many others, is tribalizing.

Kipnis: When I say "egalitarian project," I mean architecture has given up its relationship to a constituency. Only two professions use the word "constituency": architecture and politics. You know there's something wrong when that's the case. Architects don't serve a constituency and never have. It's banal to imagine a normative constituency. How we could mobilize matter, how we could design, how we could build, and where the money came from meant we served power, which then defined constituency. So it appeared for a long time that we were serving broad values, because broad values were represented by institutional powers like royalty or the church. We have just been through a period in the last thirty years — I am convinced, in retrospect — that will go down in the history books as the most important period in architecture, not for the reception of its quality but because there was more money, more power to build, more power to design, and more desire for it to happen than in the entire Renaissance or Baroque. Eight families paid for the Renaissance and Baroque; billions and billions of dollars went into the last thirty years. Part of that experiment has been a shift of attention to increasingly small audiences. It's very much like the music industry. By being successful in its model of politics, it has become either apolitical or political exactly as Bob suggests: aesthetically as opposed to singing songs about setting people free. Whether architecture should take up that experiment or not — the question of whether it's a worthwhile experiment — is being determined now.

Whiting: The analogy to the music industry doesn't hold, because the music industry produces those genres and manages them from outside. People may cross genres but they're nevertheless streamlined into identifiable genres in whatever remains of the music store today.

Kipnis: Not anymore. But you're right, they did. I have three hundred genres in my music collection.

Whiting: But they are labeled. In architecture they aren't.

Kipnis: The field has already started its atomization. There's not an infinite number, but there's perhaps two-dozen practice types that would be fairly easy to identify. As a discipline, we are still vested in the fact that we have to do good and we therefore maintain a dialectic of judgment. Considered opinion is a far more powerful tool, socially. It's much better to give an opinion and present it as a consideration than to arrive at a judgment, because a judgment is supposed to have a compelling quality outside of the passions that guide it. *Judgments* are supposed to be objective in some sense. *Genres* call for considered argumentation and compelling opinions.

Steele: Genre has been used to organize a field like film since its outset. But there's a genius that's very different than the one you're referring to, which is the genius of a Kubrick or the Coen brothers that demonstrates the facile ability to move across genres. That seems to be the challenge for architects.

Kipnis: What students should get out of that comment is the project of going through every genre. Joyce Carol Oates has made a project of writing a novel in every genre. The difference is something like this: Modern painting decided to enter a moral dialectic between abstraction and representation. It was heroic and incredible and epic; there's no question about it. And it failed. When Warhol starts doing the soup cans and the portraits he restores genre, because genre painting mobilizes more resources from the discipline than an ethical or even an intellectual dialectic. We're better off this way, although it won't feel like it. What Bob is saying about schools is probably right. If I were creating an architecture school today, I would make sure that you would know what you're going to get when you study there.

Steele: But genres are better business models; that's their power. For example, my son is a death-metal musician, among other things.

Kipnis: He's an old guy then?

Steele: It's an old genre. He is adamant about what that means. I sent him an article from *The New Yorker* where they describe it and he said it was all bullshit.

Kipnis: Yes. Hysterical exaggeration is the definition of intelligence in a genre.

Steele: But it means that when he makes his CDs, he has a business model and an established audience. And that works very well. If he wasn't in a genre, he wouldn't have that possibility.

The world I'm trying to catch an architectural school up to is a world in which it needn't any longer be a site of branding and certainty in the sense that Jeff just argued it. "I know what I'm going to get when I get there," is the model that drives the fine-tuning of offices, all kinds of worlds, and certain critical projects. One of the interesting things about schools in our moment of radical tribalization is that you can create the conditions of open warfare, such that a director like myself needn't do anything other than proliferate the possible venues or platforms for the battles to be fought. At this particular moment in the evolution of those things we think of as schools, one of their most interesting potentials is to not fall into that late-modern definition of continuity and institutional certainty. That's what I think we can learn from the unexpected, accidental, unfortunate, and often ugly consequences of those other platforms.

Kipnis: I don't see how you can teach that way. I can see how you can direct that way.

Steele: You can bring in a group of a hundred and twenty teachers to compete. It's a fifty-year-old model. Alvin Boyarsky fine-tuned it. In the first great wave of mobility, the world's first long haul destination was Heathrow. It allowed you to bring bodies together in an unprecedented way and it cracked open what was, at that point, a very stable conception of architectural education.

Whiting: But I'm struck — having watched the AA for two years now at the final evaluations — by the continuity and predictability. There's a lot of variety, but not one-hundred-and-twenty varieties. There are certain strains and some of those strains are very nostalgic. As Director, how do you affect the strains, weed out weak strains, and ensure the livelihood of strong strains? It's surprising, particularly in a market-driven model, to see how hard it is to introduce anything new.

Bob Somol: It comes down to how you view a school. When Brett showed images and said, "I'm the cameraman behind the picture," he's saying, "I'm not really in the picture." Because of the chairs and directors and deans that I've witnessed, I believe in an *auteur* model for a school. You're like a film director and there's lots of parts but there has to be a signature that's insisted upon, because left to its own devices it's going to go every which way. It does, no matter what, even with an *auteur*. So the question is: How do you at least shift it slightly this way because the weight is going elsewhere? I couldn't live with the neoliberal market model because that's already the reality and it's not hard to follow that reality when you're isomorphically mimicking the market. The issue is how to set up an alternative, which requires an *auteur* — not because you want to be an *auteur*, but because that's what the role demands.

Lavin: There's something I find incredibly interesting but also a little disconcerting in the discussion: we're talking about schools. It takes me back to Bob's notion of the speech act and Saussure and the question: What is the object of study? I didn't realize that it was institutions, which is a slightly different order of business. We're spending a lot of time talking about schools. And by talking about business models and branding for those schools there is a suggestion that we're talking about institutions or even corporations. We ought to return to speech acts, to consider what the object of study is and, more specifically, consider the question of language and genre. Is it useful to talk about *langue* and *parole* and to think about genre as a question of *parole* — with each of our schools as a particular system of utterance in the larger structure of language? Perhaps the object of criticism needs to change.

Somol: I'm also hoping to get off the topic of schools. Jeff brought in the idea of teaching. He breaks down genius and turns it into digestible, teachable parts. I think we might have a different role as critic. There are undervalued practices out there. My interest lies in how you can break those down and understand the derivative of one of them, meaning not the whole practice but one piece of it, which might actually be more valuable than the whole practice. And how do we reassemble the derivatives of practices that aren't currently in the canon, or on exhibition, or in all the publications and make a project from that? You have to take practices and do something else with them.

Lavin: But don't you then institute failure, because that's the underdog model. You're valuing the thing not because of some intrinsic character but because of its lack of value — which, I would add, as a minor art-historical note, is exactly what genre was; by definition, *genre* was the production of work that was undervalued. But, in both of those cases, it's an oblique view: you select as your object of study nothing about the object as such but rather its relation to a system of value that is produced by an external marketplace. As long as it's not in a show and not in this and not in that — none of which are decisions you've made, but have been made by others, like curators and magazine editors — it leaves whatever is left as the thing to be valued.

Somol: Not automatically. You don't just value that which is undervalued. You say there's a reason why the market isn't valuing something that actually does have a value and by recombination we can extract the value that the market doesn't see.

Kipnis: I firmly believe architecture students come to architecture school expecting to be taught how to do certain things. Mostly, they're hoping there'll be secret things like you teach magicians. Instead, we teach architecture as a mystical phenomenon. Students are confused by this mysticism and don't feel like they're learning anything. They think they don't understand what's being told to them or why they're being told. So they have no sense that they can say anything. I have yet to meet a student that said, "I came to school to learn how to do these great things and I learned." Architecture is not mystical. It's quite simple. Just think about the effect of a staircase. What happens when I go up a staircase? Why is there a big door at a church? There are long histories to these effects and then there are short-lived effects. Sylvia is the theorist of short-lived phenomenon. That's something we need to be concerned about and part of the problem is that we teach architecture as if there's a science to it. I challenge anyone to produce an effect in architecture that's based on science.

Albert Pope: I'm stuck on your idea of breaking down genius into something that's reducible and teachable. I'm thinking of the fawning students at Taliesin around Wright. One of the biggest agents of confusion in schools is the idea of genius.

Kipnis: Does music disavow its geniuses? Does physics disavow its geniuses? Does painting disavow its geniuses? We're petty and dismiss the accomplishments of architects. Instead, we claim things like the Bilbao Effect. Nobody meant that to be a positive effect. Did nobody notice the Leaning Tower of Pisa Effect hundreds of years earlier? We absolutely loathe our geniuses. We don't want to teach anybody what they do. I swear that I can take a class and teach them how to do Frank Lloyd Wright in ten weeks. Frank Lloyd Wright didn't do that.

Pope: Are there criteria aside from mystification that come from genius? Is there someone who makes decisions in a way that is intuitive or instinctive but otherwise not discursive? I don't want to make the opposite case that we want to somehow follow the human or the natural sciences and use scientific methodology. There's an alternative between the scientific method, which only sees quantities, and what we're interested in: qualities that can't be measured like science is measured. But I think there's something between the banality of the measurable and the completely subjective disciplinary notions placed on genius. I'm wondering what that would be and what category of knowledge that is. It stands apart from the scientific method but is more explicit than something like genius. I was going to follow up on the idea of fiction: storytelling, craft, art. I love storytelling. It's something that is, in some ways, quite teachable. It's explicit. And it seems to lie in the right direction: decision making that is not genius and is not the scientific method.

Kipnis: I'm saying two things: Firstly, there is such a thing as talent. You cannot teach talent. Talent occasionally rises to genius. You certainly can't teach genius. But you can mobilize knowledge, technique — disciplinary expertise — in such a way that those things grow. And, secondly, you will always measure the effectiveness of your teaching by disciplinary expertise. That's the way our discipline is driven; that's the way all disciplines are driven.

Somol: Wouldn't you prefer to say there are great projects as opposed to great people?

Kipnis: Yes. I don't care about the people.

Somol: Alright, so let's take genius off the table: My reservations about the archive translate to the reservations I have about those in the mass media that snidely dismiss the starchitect because they hate design and they hate architecture. But that's not a defense of genius. I'm interested in agency, not hypothesizing genius as the essential fount from which greatness derives. I'm more interested in the question of how we operate, and ultimately the forms of criticism and mass journalism that destroy the starchitect are really against agency. And the archive is another way to camouflage agency, such that those who recuperate the archive also don't, in my terms, take a stand. For me, the question is: How do we operate as agents?

Consistent in my work, however, has been the collapse of elite and popular forms: mass culture and modernism, the avant-garde and kitsch. I'm interested in marshaling popular examples to make room for unpopular disciplinary options. Sometimes it requires inverting hierarchies that haven't been considered. The question I would throw to Brett, Sylvia, and Jeff is: Where does your agency or your signature come from? What makes your decisions possible?

Lavin: There's a problem with the historical tradition of judgment. It produces and provokes assertions that are made too strongly. Their rhetorical form — their agency as utterances — is so bold that its effects are designed to suck all other options out of the room. I find that performance of judgment judgmental and depressing.

Bob, you're consistently able to spell out — almost masquerade in a certain way — a deeply cynical project as a projective one. It works every time. I can't help but want to follow you down a path where I'm going to discover that I'm a lemming and fall off a cliff. Suppose you figure your mode of utterance, your performative, your shifter, and all those techniques that you describe and Jeff performs; let's say you produce the effect of "I thee wed" or "You're guilty"; then there's another question that arises: "What does it mean to be married for the next fifty years?" or "What does it mean to be on death row?" It would be difficult to be as assertive about how that might operate and the effects that those conditions, once they've been uttered and once they have been called into being, might provoke.

I'm interested in those things because I believe architecture — unlike physics and other more and less scientific pursuits — plays a role in producing our subjectivity. One of the jobs of criticism is to reveal again and again how that happens and how it can happen in many different ways. So while, as a pedagogical tool, it's absolutely useful to explain to students what it means to walk up a flight of stairs or to look at how a building sits on the ground, I would, in my own mind, never imagine that walking up stairs produces the same effect every time. As a teacher, I need to open for the student the possibility of thinking about moving up stairs as something other than locomotion. But I would not want to over-determine by suggesting that walking up stairs is always going to be the same. I would want to be careful that I had some sense not only that each stair was different but also that each moment of walking on a stair would be different. For me the political agency of the critic produces a sense of possibility about who those subjects might be.

Whiting: I'm very interested in the variety that can emerge from that position, but how does one avoid relativism? Avoiding relativism requires a degree of certainty, or confidence, at a particular moment.

Lavin: I would say it's beyond certain. At any moment it's absolute. But the articulation — the utterance — has to be accompanied by the anxiety, if you will, that, at some level of knowledge, the next moment is going to be different.

Somol: I think I'd agree with that, but without the anxiety. I still think what we're discussing is our criteria for either writing, or design, or teaching, or institution building. My criterion is the logic of the joke. It doesn't require writing or architecture to be explicitly funny, but it has to obey the logic of starting with A and getting B. The logic of the joke is that somehow you were on one path and all of a sudden you wound up somewhere else. I want the world to always provoke that kind of surprise. I want it in writing and I want it in design. It's a political aesthetic project.

Lars Lerup: There's a baseline for walking up a stair and maybe there is another level where there's collusion between the subject and the stair that gives an opportunity for a completely different experience. It's that baseline that we, as agents of architecture, ought to be able to capture, but then allow for the collusion between subject and architecture to take place.

Kipnis: There's a difference between the technique of pedagogy and the sociology you're discussing. I teach with absolute certainty and demand fealty. If you want to discuss it, wait until you finish my class. You can discuss it later, but, when you're in my class, you do it. I expect maturity and judgment to grow out of this naïve certainty.

Roberts: The challenge facing this generation of students and emerging practitioners is that they are coming of age after multiple generations have dissolved the agency of the individual subject. What seems to be missing in the discussion is how you talk about the choices you make as an individual making something. A lot of the discussion has been about fiction as a way of carving out our own worlds within this larger world. But the challenge is how you believe in that world while having a critical awareness of what we can't possibly ignore, which is this larger context of the subject. It's rare that we explain the choices we make, because we're still leaning on external explanations.

Kipnis: This idea of a complete poststructuralist disassembly of the Self is just not true. That's not your personal experience. That's not anybody's personal experience. Your generation forms more mobile groups. Your sociology is different. But there's still will. You still live in a Proustian world. You have to recognize that there are — and Bob put this very clearly

— possibilities and limitations in architecture and you're looking at a world in which authentic communities are based more on remote exchange than on proximate exchange. I don't care who lives next door and I don't want to meet them; but I can't wait to get on Facebook. Then you have to design a building that sits still somewhere. Do I think that's an intractable problem? No, I think it's a simple problem because there's an architectural history of it: datum, field, urban field, cosmopolitan field. There's a history that architecture has already produced on how to deal with the authenticity of remote communities in local situations given architecture is immobile. And if you know that history, you also know your possibilities and your limitations and you are encouraged to add to that history. But if you're just constantly befuddled by the fact that you don't see any relationship between your work and the world around you, I don't see how you can possibly work at all.

Roberts: But I think there's a real contradiction in what you're saying. You talk about the discipline as a shared set of rules that we can all follow and that has great continuity over time, but then you also talk about the genius of people who were able to transform that discipline. So how do we make those choices to break the rules?

Kipnis: That's the point. Not one time will I ask you to break a rule. I will punish you for breaking a rule, so that when you break a rule you know why you're breaking it.

Interview II

Brett Steele

Sam Biroscak, Mary Casper, Chimaobi Izeogu, Sean Billy Kizy, Mahan Shirazi, Alex Tehranian

Mary Casper: You were saying how interesting you think the work of editors is today.

Brett Steele: Editors have shaped architecture in profound ways, as much or more than architectural work in the traditional sense. Modern architecture wasn't invented by putting steel and glass together. Between 1917 and 1926, when there was little of that activity, there was an editorial imagination that shaped arguments about the urgency of doing that.

Sean Billy Kizy: Would you say architecture is as much editing as invention?

Steele: Editing is a hugely influential aspect of contemporary design. Contemporary design tools produce an internal history within projects that require an editorial command that we're still struggling to articulate and understand. We're all becoming librarians of our own lives.

Kizy: Are you creating narratives and stories in your role as director of the AA?

Steele: Absolutely. That's all I was doing today. I'll go to a different town next week and I'll tell a different story. You're testing different descriptions to see what works and what doesn't. Some parts are interesting to me and will stick; I'll work on other parts; and I'll carve other parts away. You're trying to come up with accounts for the world. It's not a question of whether these things are true or false. It's the recognition that stories shape the world; they're more real than reality. Storytelling is the dominant technology of your generation. Stories construct identities for brands. Stories are the way we write the history of projects. When you stand up in a jury you're crafting and constructing an account of how this project came together the way it did. It's neither real nor unreal, but a construction.

Alex Tehranian: As the Director of the AA, do you think your role is to curate the different interests you bring into the school? Do you think your role is to direct the bias of your students? Or do you think your role is to set up an open platform that is less directed?

Steele: My position is not entirely neutral; it doesn't espouse a free-for-all, to see who lives or dies. Even the most right-winged, economic accounts of the market recognize the utility of "market mechanisms" that stabilize fluctuations and allow forces to play out over time. When I bring someone in, I don't throw them to the lions. They know their position depends on their ability to articulate and communicate an argument to an audience. They sometimes need time to find their form. Part of my job is to carve out a space and provide the time for something to work or not.

Tehranian: Do you put forward an agenda?

Steele: Absolutely. My job depends upon keeping the confidence of the school. The question is how you do that without becoming a politician.

Casper: You talk about how the school brings together different voices, but the AA books have such a consistent, recognizable, and distinct style that brands the school in a certain way. Do you think the style stands for something?

Steele: I don't personally intend it to mean anything. I have a brilliant team that does this. It's deliberately not run through the school. We felt the need for the series to provide enough continuity of form to enable very different content to relate. The publications are not neutral. They have a consistent space within which difference can be measured and compared. And, in a way, that's also what happens in the school. The studios have a consistent form — twelve students and two or three teachers — in which otherwise entirely different design units play out.

Mahan Shirazi: How would you describe the global satellite schools of the AA?

Steele: The satellite schools are the opposite of my normal world which exists in eight historically important buildings in London. It's a very old, traditional, stable, ordinary, yet well-known terrain. The visiting schools are an opportunity for the

AA to experiment with different kinds of spaces — spaces that we have for eight or ten days at a time, sometimes longer, in places we don't know, in places we don't own, with people we don't know.

Kizy: Is there something consistent that makes it the AA everywhere?

Steele: Only that the people involved are in some way associated with the AA, although at different levels of experience. There isn't an agenda that ties it all together, because the nature of each particular project requires the person directing that group to take the lead. It's similar to the way the school works: these courses are shaped around individual team agendas.

Shirazi: It seems like the AA is not just a school for students, but a school for instructors, allowing them to come up with new stories.

Steele: Yes, new arguments, ideas, and agendas. Absolutely. Having been a student, a teacher, a graduate program director, and a director of the school, by far the hardest role — and this is the case for many who have been through it — is the teaching role. It's warfare. You're up against peers that are often hard for you to figure out, because they're doing something you didn't know existed as a possibility. At the AA you're not hired to deliver a particular kind of course; you have to deliver a compelling agenda that is communicated clearly enough that people can react to it.

Sam Biroscak: Do you see the unconventional structure of the AA show up in your students' work?

Steele: I see it in the portfolios, absolutely. We're at the early stage of the portfolio reviews, which document the year's work and are built up as the project unfolds. You're ultimately assessing whether the portfolio demonstrates a critical awareness of what it contains — where the learning occurred and where it didn't — and if you've got that, you're done. I don't think a school should ever be more complicated than that.

Biroscak: It's an intentional lack of overall narrative?

Steele: It's a narrative of non-uniformity between the different tribes that make up the bigger machine.

Kizy: Do you curate conversations between the tribes?

Steele: Part of my job is to get people out of their silos, as I call them. That's one of the things that makes schools different than other spaces right now. They have the capacity to bring together groups that don't have the ability to talk to one another. That's something the school considers hugely important and, it should be said, it's often where some of the biggest disasters take place.

Interview III

Jeffrey Kipnis

Mary Casper, Sean Billy Kizy, Alex Tehranian

Mary Casper: Does a genius know the discipline better than others?

Jeffrey Kipnis: I said there was genius, not *a* genius. Einstein wasn't *a* genius. The contributions he made to the discussion were very small by the time he made them. A lot of people had been working on the subject for a long time. He made a leap and that leap was a leap of genius. It didn't make him a genius. There's no such thing as a genius. But there is a culture of acts of genius that organize every discipline. You can't teach it, but you can enable it. Einstein didn't learn physics from a really special teacher, who taught him something nobody else knew. And he couldn't have done what he did had he not learned physics.

Casper: How do you think narrative relates to architecture?

Kipnis: It's not so much the story itself as the way each discipline tells stories that's important. For example, you know when a book starts and when it ends and you basically know how long it lasts. It has a strong curtain rising — a strong beginning — it has a strong ending, and it has a strong duration. The problem for most novelists is a strong ending, because after you've spent fifteen to thirty hours reading a story, even if it's a comedy, the end is going to make you feel like it died. One of the difficulties for any novelist is figuring out how to end a book without leaving the reader remorseful. So, how does a painting begin?

Casper: With a brushstroke?

Kipnis: I didn't ask you how to write a book; I asked you what happened when you read a book. When you see a painting, how do you know when to start? I think you have no idea how paintings start; I think you have no idea how they end; and I don't think you have any idea how long they last. Paintings have weak beginnings and weak endings and indeterminate durations. Does a building have a strong beginning?

Casper: I think it does. It has a front door.

Kipnis: Virtually every description of architecture you've learned, from issues of façade, to architectural promenade, to *piano nobile*, to relationship to context — every value judgment you have — has a strong beginning about the architecture. Now, do they have strong endings?

Casper: No.

Kipnis: That's right. Buildings have a very strong beginning; they have very weak endings. Otherwise you'd feel like you'd died every time you left a building. There's not a single building I know that is famous for the celebration of its exit. Because it has to be a weak experience. *All* narratives of architecture are shaped by these disciplinary characteristics of curtain rising, duration, and termination.

Alex Tehranian: How does representation of the building play into that experience? If you've never experienced a building, but you've seen it in photographs or drawings, does that change the experience?

Kipnis: There's no encounter that's free of the effects of representation. There is no phenomenological experience outside of cultural context.

Casper: What is the relationship?

Kipnis: There are multiple relationships: the book represents the movie; the movie represents the life of the character; the character represents people in that context. But there is also the way the movie is completely different from the book and its original. It re-originates the book. You get a dual scheme of representation and re-origination, in which every discipline participates with every other discipline in the economics of those exchanges.

Casper: Do you think there's any primacy to the original?

Kipnis: The copy constructs the original as the original. It doesn't make it any less original; it doesn't undermine its status as an original. Everything has qualities of representing something and will be represented by something else, but it also has irreducible and irreproducible qualities that are not available to paraphrase. After you think about it for a while, it's going to be the way you want the world to be.

Sean Billy Kizy: Why will focusing our attention on architecture's long-lived problems prevent us from becoming a "boutique specialization"?

Kipnis: Boutique specialists consider the performance of a building. That has nothing to do with architecture. It's true that architects also consider the performance of a building, but that will not be their primary consideration. As soon as that becomes their primary consideration, they're no longer architects; they're building type specialists. That's an okay thing to be. I'm okay if you want to be a developer; I'm okay if you want to be an engineer; I'm okay if you want to be a hobbyist builder. All these people have the right to use buildings in their own disciplines. When you sit at a table as an architect — let's say there are ten people at the table: there's an engineer, a psychologist, a financier, a mayor, etc. — what are you going to say that you know none of the others know? If you tell me your job is to coordinate things as a generalist, you're dead. So what area of expertise do you have that they have no other idea about? It's the architectural effects of buildings. It's nothing mystical; it's nothing arcane; it's nothing mysterious. You know the effects of buildings because you've studied them and you've studied their changes over time and the way they affect peoples lives, other than the direct performance of the building as such.

Kizy: So the qualitative and not the quantitative.

Kipnis: You say that as if it's pejorative, but every decision you make in your life is based on qualities as opposed to quantities. I think we live in a phenomic world, not a genomic world. We make decisions based on affects, qualities, and the stories that include them. It's not an area of judgment; it's an area of opinion.

Tehranian: How do you prevent something typical from becoming a cliché?

Kipnis: Clichés are good things, but you have to find alternatives to threadbare clichés that are no longer doing their job. If you set out to break every cliché, you're finished. Clichés are simply reliable patterns of performance. A building type is a cliché. A palazzo is a cliché. A two-bedroom house is a cliché. There's nothing wrong with clichés. You can get tired of something. It's perfectly legitimate to see so many glass box buildings that you're just tired of it. That's a point where clichés become overbearing or threadbare and no longer have the power they were originally intended to have.

Kizy: What is hindering our knowledge?

Kipnis: To begin with, architects often don't believe there is any architectural knowledge. It's not scientific in nature, it's art-like in nature; but that is just as reliable. We live our lives on the basis of art-like stories, not scientific-like conclusions.

Tehranian: There's common knowledge that we can understand and use, but you're also suggesting we have to be able to think through the cliché and understand its implications rather than just accepting it at face value.

Kipnis: If you don't learn the discipline, you will simply repeat its clichés to the point of tedium. The problem with clichés is not having alternatives. Contemporary work makes older work contemporary again. Rem's work has made Mies's work contemporary in a way that Mies had no understanding of at all.

Casper: Is that re-origination?

Kipnis: Yes, exactly; it's the idea that the copy produces the original as the original. I'm not asking for everybody to change the world with every building. Ninety-nine percent of the decisions you make in the design of a building are made for you. That is true for any art form. There's a little movement and you have to be deeply knowledgeable about the possibilities of those movements. But, because it's art, your knowledge isn't about repeating them; it's about keeping them alive by moving them.

Tehranian: Do you think we should spend more time studying antecedents, breaking them down to understand specifically what they're doing?

Kipnis: What else do you study? If you don't have historical knowledge, what you do in the studio is going to be historical knowledge of a really trivial kind. It's up to you and your teachers to create a canon. In every period canons will change and particular groups will change canons, but, in the end, you'll know more by studying the discipline as a discipline. It's not about history per se. I don't care what happened, when, and why. Although it's powerful to know those contexts so we operate better today. If you really want to be a funny comic today, you better know the history of comedy, but you better not re-tell it. If you don't know it, how do you grow from it?

Interview IV

Sylvia Lavin

Mary Casper, Maia Simon

Mary Casper: Could you talk about your recent travel, following Bernard Rudofsky's *Architecture Without Architects*. How would you characterize lower-case "a" architecture now compared with capital "A" architecture? Do you have a preference for "raw" over "cooked" architecture?

Sylvia Lavin: The idea of the raw and the cooked was largely an opportunity to historicize the contemporary interest in experience and the various forms of naturalism circulating today. Going to these strange sites from Rudofsky's book was an elaborate ruse to think through those issues. The sites we went to were not raw in the sense he imagined. I don't have any particular interest in those sites as such. I was trying to disabuse my students of the expectation that going to a site would fill them with certainty. I'm interested in dislodging the notion that going to a site has intrinsic truth-value. I'm concerned when architectural ideas are converted into certainties. Issues like affect and atmosphere started as modes of speculation but have increasingly obtained a reactionary undertone that concerns me.

Casper: What do you mean by "certainty"?

Lavin: I would say it's how we rethink Stella's expression, "What you see is what you see." When that sentence was first uttered, it was a rhetorical evacuation of external references from painting. It had a specific job to do. It meant: "Don't look for meaning." "Don't look for signs and symbols." "What you see is what you get." That's what it meant. When people say that today, they're not engaged in the same project. Today, "What you see is what you get" is being used for purposes that are both intellectually expansive and intellectually limiting. I like the expansive part; I don't like the limiting part. When Stella said that — and there is a huge amount of art and architectural criticism rooted in that historical moment — the observer was a very particular, universalized subject. I don't think we can accept that subject anymore. And if we don't, the certainty of the chain between what you see and what you get has to be undone. Architecture is currently reconsidering this issue from many different points of view. People are returning to the question you asked me, namely what is the difference between architecture with a capital "A" and architecture with a lower-case "a"? I'm curious about that distinction because, at least as I understand it, that distinction is usually made between the term "architecture" and "building." A lot of discourses are invested in new ways of exploring the "building" side of the equation today: materialism, patterns of construction, assemblage, parametric design. Building is the repository for this notion of "What you see is what you get," because the complex representational things that mean that what you see is not what you get, or you can't even see what you get, are on the architecture side of the equation.

Maia Simon: Where do you exercise judgment in your practice?

Lavin: I believe in the notion of an immanent critique. Certain kinds of projects set up their own rules and it is, in part, my job as judge to try to understand if the rules set by the project have been followed. So I insist on a particular kind of accountability, although I would like to think it doesn't appear judgmental because I try to maintain openness to otherwise incompatible practices.

Casper: How does your judgment as a critic come into tension with the bias or the judgment of the architect, or the bias or the judgment of a multiplicity of subjects? Would you consider your judgment to be one instance of the multitude of subjectivities, or are you somewhere in-between?

Lavin: Isn't the real question: Do I consider my judgment to be better than that of others? Yes.

Casper: On what do you base that authority?

Lavin: Hubris!

Simon: Do you see judgment as separate from taste or dependent on taste? Are there criteria for judgment beyond your personal criteria?

Lavin: Yes. I believe judgment is the effect of rhetorical precision. Like all good forms of rhetoric, its efficacy is measured in the degree to which it convinces the receiver of its truth-value. That does not mean it has truth-value. It has the effect of truth-value. I do believe judgment is a rhetorical, and, in my case, primarily, but not exclusively, writerly practice.

Casper: What would you identify as your specific bias?

Lavin: I feel the need to resist use of the term "bias" because of the connotation of self-delusion. Generally one uses "bias" to suggest an orientation in one direction for no good reason, and ultimately, for reasons of which the biased person is not even aware. I think it's important for a critic to be acutely aware of the interaction between their sense of experience and their knowledge of their own historical construction as a subject. I do it in particular ways: I find it most productive to interrogate architecture in relation to other things.

Casper: Would it be accurate to say your bias is concerned with the boundaries between the disciplines of art, history, popular culture, and architecture?

Lavin: I wouldn't put it that way. I would say I find those creases in the cultural field to be moments of great potential for exercising judgment, which I consider to be a form of constructing plausible truths.

Casper: What do you mean when you say "truth"?

Lavin: Anything that makes you nod your head. I use it in a deliberately false way.

Casper: Who in architecture today deserves the right to judge?